IN THIS OUR

CHARLOTTE PERKINS GILMAN

SCIRE·QVOD
SCIENDVM

WOULD YE BUT UNDERSTAND!
   JOY IS ON EVERY HAND!
YE SHUT YOUR EYES AND CALL IT NIGHT,
YE GROPE AND FALL IN SEAS OF LIGHT—
   WOULD YE BUT UNDERSTAND.

CONTENTS.

CONTENTS.

CONTENTS.

CONTENTS.

WOMAN

THE WORLD.

BIRTH.

Lord, I am born!
I have built me a body
Whose ways are all open,
Whose currents run free,
From the life that is thine
Flowing ever within me,
To the life that is mine
Flowing outward through me.

I am clothed, and my raiment
Fits smooth to the spirit,
The soul moves unhindered,
The body is free;
And the thought that my body
Falls short of expressing,
In texture and color
Unfoldeth on me.

I am housed, O my Father!
My body is sheltered,
My spirit has room
'Twixt the whole world and me,
I am guarded with beauty and strength,
And within it
Is room for still union,
And birth floweth free.

1

And the union and birth
Of the house, ever growing,
Have built me a city —
Have born me a state —
Where I live manifold,
Many-voiced, many-hearted,
Never dead, never weary,
And oh ! never parted !
The life of The Human,
So subtle — so great !

Lord, I am born !
From inmost to outmost
The ways are all open,
The currents run free,
From thy voice in my soul
To my joy in the people —
I thank thee, O God,
For this body thou gavest,
Which enfoldeth the earth —
Is enfolded by thee !

NATURE'S ANSWER.

I.

A MAN would build a house, and found a place
As fair as any on the earth's fair face :

2

Soft hills, dark woods, smooth meadows richly green,
And cool tree-shaded lakes the hills between.

He built his house within this pleasant land,
A stately white-porched house, long years to stand;

But, rising from his paradise so fair,
Came fever in the night and killed him there.

"O lovely land!" he cried, "how could I know
That death was lurking under this fair show?"

And answered Nature, merciful and stern,
"I teach by killing; let the others learn!"

II.

A man would do great work, good work and true;
He gave all things he had, all things he knew;

He worked for all the world; his one desire
To make the people happier, better, higher;

Used his best wisdom, used his utmost strength;
And, dying in the struggle, found at length,

The giant evils he had fought the same,
And that the world he loved scarce knew his name.

"Has all my work been wrong? I meant so well!
I loved so much!" he cried. "How could I tell?"

And answered Nature, merciful and stern,
"I teach by killing; let the others learn."

3

III.

A maid was asked in marriage. Wise as fair,
She gave her answer with deep thought and prayer,

Expecting, in the holy name of wife,
Great work, great pain, and greater joy, in life.

She found such work as brainless slaves might do,
By day and night, long labor, never through;

Such pain — no language can her pain reveal;
It had no limit but her power to feel;

Such joy — life left in her sad soul's employ
Neither the hope nor memory of joy.

Helpless, she died, with one despairing cry, —
"I thought it good; how could I tell the lie?"

And answered Nature, merciful and stern,
"I teach by killing; let the others learn."

THE COMMONPLACE.

LIFE is so weary commonplace! Too fair
Were those young visions of the poet and seer.
Nothing exciting ever happens here.
Just eat and drink, and dress and chat;
Life is so tedious, slow, and flat,
And every day alike in everywhere!

4

Birth comes.   Birth —
The breathing re-creation of the earth!
All earth, all sky, all God, life's deep sweet whole,
Newborn again to each new soul!
"Oh, are you?   What a shame!   Too bad, my dear!
How well you stand it, too!   It's very queer
The dreadful trials women have to carry;
But you can't always help it when you marry.
Oh, what a sweet layette!   What lovely socks!
What an exquisite puff and powder box!
Who is your doctor?   Yes, his skill's immense —
But it's a dreadful danger and expense!"

Love comes.   Love —
And the world widens at the touch thereof;
Deepens and lightens till the answer true
To all life's questions seems to glimmer through.
"Engaged?   I knew it must be!   What a ring!
Worth how much?   Well, you are a lucky thing!
But how was Jack disposed of?"   "Jack?   Oh, he
Was just as glad as I was to be free.
You might as well ask after George and Joe
And all the fellows that I used to know!
I don't inquire for his past Kate and Carry —
Every one's pleased.   It's time, you know, to
    marry."

Life comes.   Life —
Bearing within it wisdom, work, and strife.

To do, to strive, to know, and, with the knowing,
To find life's widest purpose in our growing.
"How are you, Jim? Pleasant weather to-day!
How's business?" "Well, it does n't come my
  way."
"Good-morning, Mrs. Smith! I hope you 're well!
Tell me the news!" "The news? There 's none to
  tell.
The cook has left; the baby 's got a tooth;
John has gone fishing to renew his youth.
House-cleaning 's due — or else we 'll have to move!
How sweet you are in that! Good-bye, my love!"

Death comes. Death —
Love cries to love, and no man answereth.
Death the beginning, Death the endless end,
Life 's proof and first condition, Birth's best friend.
"Yes, it 's a dreadful loss! No coming back!
Never again! How do I look in black?
And then he suffered so! Oh, yes, we all
Are well provided for. You 're kind to call,
And Mrs. Green has lost her baby too!
Dear me! How sad! And yet what could they do?
With such a hard time as they have, you know, —
No doubt 't was better for the child to go!"

Life is so dreary commonplace. We bear
One dull yoke, in the country or the town.
We 're born, grow up, marry, and settle down.

I used to think — but then a man must live!
The Fates dole out the weary years they give,
And every day alike in everywhere.

HOMES.

A SESTINA.

WE are the smiling comfortable homes
With happy families enthroned therein,
Where baby souls are brought to meet the world,
Where women end their duties and desires,
For which men labor as the goal of life,
That people worship now instead of God.

Do we not teach the child to worship God? —
Whose soul's young range is bounded by the homes
Of those he loves, and where he learns that life
Is all constrained to serve the wants therein,
Domestic needs and personal desires, —
These are the early limits of his world.

And are we not the woman's perfect world,
Prescribed by nature and ordained of God,
Beyond which she can have no right desires,
No need for service other than in homes?
For doth she not bring up her young therein?
And is not rearing young the end of life?

And man? What other need hath he in life
Than to go forth and labor in the world,

7

And struggle sore with other men therein?
Not to serve other men, nor yet his God,
But to maintain these comfortable homes, —
The end of all a normal man's desires.

Shall not the soul's most measureless desires
Learn that the very flower and fruit of life
Lies all attained in comfortable homes,
With which life's purpose is to dot the world
And consummate the utmost will of God,
By sitting down to eat and drink therein.

Yea, in the processes that work therein —
Fulfilment of our natural desires —
Surely man finds the proof that mighty God
For to maintain and reproduce his life
Created him and set him in the world;
And this high end is best attained in homes.

Are we not homes? And is not all therein?
Wring dry the world to meet our wide desires!
We crown all life! We are the aim of God!

A COMMON INFERENCE.

A NIGHT: mysterious, tender, quiet, deep;
Heavy with flowers; full of life asleep;
Thrilling with insect voices; thick with stars;

8

No cloud between the dewdrops and red Mars;
The small earth whirling softly on her way,
The moonbeams and the waterfalls at play;
A million million worlds that move in peace,
A million mighty laws that never cease;
And one small ant-heap, hidden by small weeds,
Rich with eggs, slaves, and store of millet seeds.
        They sleep beneath the sod
            And trust in God.

A day: all glorious, royal, blazing bright;
Heavy with flowers; full of life and light;
Great fields of corn and sunshine; courteous trees;
Snow-sainted mountains; earth-embracing seas;
Wide golden deserts; slender silver streams;
Clear rainbows where the tossing fountain gleams;
And everywhere, in happiness and peace,
A million forms of life that never cease;
And one small ant-heap, crushed by passing tread,
Hath scarce enough alive to mourn the dead!
        They shriek beneath the sod,
            "There is no God!"

THE ROCK AND THE SEA.

THE ROCK.

I am the Rock, presumptuous Sea!
I am set to encounter thee.

Angry and loud or gentle and still,
I am set here to limit thy power, and I will!
     I am the Rock!

I am the Rock. From age to age
I scorn thy fury and dare thy rage.
Scarred by frost and worn by time,
Brown with weed and green with slime,
Thou may'st drench and defile me and spit in my
    face,
But while I am here thou keep'st thy place!
     I am the Rock!

I am the Rock, beguiling Sea!
I know thou art fair as fair can be,
With golden glitter and silver sheen,
And bosom of blue and garments of green.
Thou may'st pat my cheek with baby hands,
And lap my feet in diamond sands,
And play before me as children play;
But plead as thou wilt, I bar the way!
     I am the Rock!

I am the Rock. Black midnight falls;
The terrible breakers rise like walls;
With curling lips and gleaming teeth
They plunge and tear at my bones beneath.
Year upon year they grind and beat
In storms of thunder and storms of sleet, —
     10

Grind and beat and wrestle and tear,
But the rock they beat on is always there
      I am the Rock!

THE SEA.

I am the Sea. I hold the land
As one holds an apple in his hand,
Hold it fast with sleepless eyes,
Watching the continents sink and rise.
Out of my bosom the mountains grow,
Back to its depths they crumble slow;
The earth is a helpless child to me.
      I am the Sea !

I am the Sea. When I draw back
Blossom and verdure follow my track,
And the land I leave grows proud and fair,
For the wonderful race of man is there;
And the winds of heaven wail and cry
While the nations rise and reign and die,
Living and dying in folly and pain,
While the laws of the universe thunder in vain.
What is the folly of man to me?
      I am the Sea.

I am the Sea. The earth I sway ;
Granite to me is potter's clay ;
Under the touch of my careless waves
It rises in turrets and sinks in caves ;
The iron cliffs that edge the land

11

I grind to pebbles and sift to sand,
And beach-grass bloweth and children play
In what were the rocks of yesterday.
It is but a moment of sport to me.
       I am the Sea!

I am the Sea. In my bosom deep
Wealth and Wonder and Beauty sleep;
Wealth and Wonder and Beauty rise
In changing splendor of sunset skies,
And comfort the earth with rains and snows
Till waves the harvest and laughs the rose.
Flower and forest and child of breath
With me have life — without me, death.
What if the ships go down in me?
       I am the Sea!

THE LION PATH.

I DARE not!
      Look! the road is very dark ;
The trees stir softly and the bushes shake,
The long grass rustles, and the darkness moves
Here — there — beyond !
There 's something crept across the road just now !
And you would have me go ?
Go *there*, through that live darkness, hideous
With stir of crouching forms that wait to kill?
Ah, *look !* See there! and there ! and there again !

Great yellow glassy eyes, close to the ground !
Look !   Now the clouds are lighter I can see
The long slow lashing of the sinewy tails,
And the set quiver of strong jaws that wait !
Go there ?   Not I !   Who dares to go who sees
So perfectly the lions in the path ?

Comes one who dares.
                    Afraid at first, yet bound
On such high errand as no fear could stay.
Forth goes he with the lions in his path.
And then — ?

            He dared a death of agony,
Outnumbered battle with the king of beasts,
Long struggle in the horror of the night,
Dared and went forth to meet — O ye who fear !
Finding an empty road, and nothing there, —
A wide, bare, common road, with homely fields,
And fences, and the dusty roadside trees —
Some spitting kittens, maybe, in the grass.

REINFORCEMENTS.

YEA, we despair.   Because the night is long,
And all arms weary with the endless fight
With blind, black forces of insulted law
Which we continually disobey,
And know not how to honor if we would.

13

How can we fight when every effort fails,
And the vast hydra looms before us still
Headed as thickly as at dawn of day,
Fierce as when evening fell on us at war?
We are aweary, and no help appears;
No light, no knowledge, no sure way to kill
Our ancient enemy.   Let us give o'er !
We do but fight with fate ! Lay down your arms !
Retreat ! Surrender ! Better live as slaves
Than fight forever on a losing field !

Hold, ye faint-hearted !   Ye are not alone !
Into your worn-out ranks of weary men
Come mighty reinforcements, even now !
Look where the dawn is kindling in the east,
Brave with the glory of the better day, —
A countless host, an endless host, all fresh,
With unstained banners and unsullied shields,
With shining swords that point to victory,
And great young hearts that know not how to
      fear, —
The Children come to save the weary world !

HEROISM.

It takes great strength to train
To modern service your ancestral brain ;
To lift the weight of the unnumbered years
Of dead men's habits, methods, and ideas ;

14

To hold that back with one hand, and support
With the other the weak steps of a new thought.

It takes great strength to bring your life up square
With your accepted thought, and hold it there;
Resisting the inertia that drags back
From new attempts to the old habit's track.
It is so easy to drift back, to sink ;
So hard to live abreast of what you think!

It takes great strength to live where you belong
When other people think that you are wrong;
People you love, and who love you, and whose
Approval is a pleasure you would choose.
To bear this pressure and succeed at length
In living your belief — well, it takes strength.

And courage too.   But what does courage mean
Save strength to help you face a pain foreseen ?
Courage to undertake this lifelong strain
Of setting yours against your grandsire's brain;
Dangerous risk of walking lone and free
Out of the easy paths that used to be,
And the fierce pain of hurting those we love
When love meets truth, and truth must ride above?

But the best courage man has ever shown
Is daring to cut loose and think alone.
Dark as the unlit chambers of clear space
Where light shines back from no reflecting face.

Our sun's wide glare, our heaven's shining blue,
We owe to fog and dust they fumble through;
And our rich wisdom that we treasure so
Shines from the thousand things that we don't know.
But to think new — it takes a courage grim
As led Columbus over the world's rim.
To think it cost some courage. And to go —
Try it. It taxes every power you know.

It takes great love to stir a human heart
To live beyond the others and apart.
A love that is not shallow, is not small,
Is not for one, or two, but for them all.
Love that can wound love, for its higher need;
Love that can leave love though the heart may bleed;
Love that can lose love; family, and friend;
Yet steadfastly live, loving, to the end.
A love that asks no answer, that can live
Moved by one burning, deathless force, — to give.
Love, strength, and courage. Courage, strength,
    and love,
The heroes of all time are built thereof.

FIRE WITH FIRE.

THERE are creeping flames in the near-by grass;
There are leaping flames afar;
And the wind's black breath

Is hot with death, —
The worst of the deaths that are !

And north is fire and south is fire,
And east and west the same ;
The sunlight chokes,
The whole earth smokes,
The only light is flame !

But what do I care for the girdle of death
With its wavering wall and spire !
I draw the ring
Where I am king,
And fight the fire with fire !

My blaze is not as wide as the world,
Nor tall for the world to see;
But the flames I make
For life's sweet sake,
Are between the fire and me.

That fire would burn in wantonness
All things that life must use;
Some things I lay
In the dragon's way
And burn because I choose.

The sky is black, the air is red,
The earth is a flaming sea ;

You must not steal nor take man's life,
You must not covet your neighbor's wife,
And woman must cling at every cost
To her one virtue, or she is lost —
  Preach about the old sins, Preacher !
  Not about the new !

  Preach about the other man, Preacher !
    The man we all can see !
The man of oaths, the man of strife,
The man who drinks and beats his wife,
Who helps his mates to fret and shirk
When all they need is to keep at work —
  Preach about the other man, Preacher !
  Not about me !

A TYPE.

I AM too little, said the Wretch,
  For any one to see.
Among the million men who do
This thing that I am doing too,
  Why should they notice me ?

My sin is common as to breathe ;
  It rests on every back.
And surely I am not to blame
Where everybody does the same, —
  Am not a bit more black !

20

And so he took his willing share
   In a universal crime,
Thinking that no reproach could fall
On one who shared the fault of all,
   Who did it all the time.

Then Genius came, and showed the world
   What thing it was they did;
How their offence had reached the poles
With stench of slain unburied souls,
   And all men cowered and hid.

Then Genius took that one poor Wretch
   For now the time was ripe;
Stripped him of every shield and blind,
And nailed him up for all mankind
   To study — as a type!

COMPROMISE.

It is well to fight and win —
   If that may be;
It is well to fight and die therein —
   For such go free;

It is ill to fight and find no grave
   But a prison-cell;
To keep alive, yet live a slave —
   Praise those who fell!

Than to be yourself as spotless as a baby one year
 old,
Your domestic habits wholly free from blame,
  While the company you stand with
  Is a thing to curse a land with,
And your public life is undiluted shame.

For the deeds men.do together are what saves the
 world to-day —
By our common public work we stand or fall —
  And your fraction of the sin
  Of the office you are in
Is the sin that 's going to damn you, after all !

OUT OF PLACE.

  CELL, poor little cell,
  Distended with pain,
  Torn with the pressure
  Of currents of effort
  Resisted in vain ;
  Feeling sweep by you
  The stream of nutrition,
  Unable to take ;
  Crushed flat and inactive,
  While shudder across you
  Great forces that wake ;
  Alone — while far voices
   24

THE WORLD.

Across all the shouting
Call you to your own ;
Held fast, fastened close,
Surrounded, enveloped,
How you starve there alone !
Cell, poor little cell,
Let the pain pass — don't hold it !
Let the effort pass through you !
Let go !   And give way !
You will find your own place ;
You will join your own people ;
See the light of your day !

Rhyme, Jdly

childlivening to it .
'little pig' little pig!

LITTLE CELL

imprisonment of our set 'place'.

LITTLE Cell !   Little Cell ! with a heart as big as
   heaven,   *spot of the face of creation*
Remember that you are but a part !   *and race —*
This great longing in your soul   *vital, yet insignificant*
Is the longing of the whole,   *to the eye.*
And your work is not done with your heart !   *Women*
   are needed .

Don't imagine, Little Cell,   *Patronising -*
That the work you do so well   *no identity — now for*
Is the only work the world needs to do !   *Purpose 'a Woman'*
You are wanted in your place
For the growing of the race ;   *a national resource →*
But the growing does not all depend on you !   *Reproduction.*

25

yearning to do More than custom pronounces necessary .

Men's patronising voice → men do the work too!

'The Body of Christ ?'

Little Cell! Little Cell! with a race's whole ambition, —*Women Race or human Race?*
Remember there are others growing, too!
You 've been noble, you 've been strong;
Rest a while and come along;
Let the world take a turn and carry you!
men as one all — we work too.

THE CHILD SPEAKS.

GET back! Give me air! Give me freedom and
room,
The warm earth and bright water, the crowding
sweet bloom
Of the flowers, and the measureless, marvellous
sky, —
All of these all the time, and a shelter close by
Where silence and beauty and peace are my own
In a chamber alone.

Then bring me the others! " A child " is a crime;
It is " children " who grow through the beautiful
time
Of their childhood up into the age you are in.
" A child " must needs suffer and sicken and
sin;
The life of a child needs the life of its kind,
O ye stupid and blind!

26

Then the best of your heart and the best of your
    brain!
The face of all beauty! The soul without stain!
Your noblest! Your wisest! With us is the place
To consecrate life to the good of the race!
That our childhood may pass with the best you
    can give,
        And our manhood so live!

The wisdom of years, the experience deep
That shall laugh with our waking and watch with
    our sleep,
The patience of age, the keen honor of youth,
To guide us in doing and teach us in truth,
With the garnered ripe fruit of the world at our feet,
        Both the bitter and sweet!

What is this that you offer? One man's narrow
    purse!
One woman's strained life, and a heart straining
    worse!
Confined as in prisons — held down as in caves —
The teaching of tyrants — the service of slaves —
The garments of falsehood and bondage — the
    weight
        Of your own evil state.

And what is this brought as atonement for these?
For our blind misdirection, our death and disease;

For the grief of our childhood, the loss and the
    wrong;
For the pain of our childhood, the agony strong;
For the shame and the sin and the sorrow thereof —
    Dare you say it is love?

Love? First give freedom, — the right of the brute!
The air with its sunshine, the earth with its fruit.
Love? First give wisdom, — intelligent care,
That shall help to bring out all the good that is
    there.
Love? First give justice! There's nothing
    above!
        And then you may love!

TO A GOOD MANY.

O BLIND and selfish! Helpless as the beast
Who sees no meaning in a soul released
And given flesh to grow in — to work through!
Think you that God has nothing else to do
Than babble endlessly the same set phrase?
Are life's great spreading, upward-reaching ways
Laid for the beasts to climb on till the top
Is reached in you, you think, and there you stop!
They were raised up, obedient to force
Which lifted them, unwitting of their course.
You have new power, new consciousness, new sight;
You can help God! You stand in the great light

Of seeing him at work. You can go on
And walk with him, and feel the glory won.
And here you sit, content to toil and strive
To keep your kind of animal alive !
Why, friends ! God is not through !
The universe is not complete in you.
You 're just as bound to follow out his plan
And sink yourself in ever-growing Man
As ever were the earliest, crudest eggs
To grow to vertebrates with arms and legs.
Society holds not its present height
Merely that you may bring a child to light ;
But you and yours live only in the plan
That 's working out a higher kind of man ;
A higher kind of life, that shall let grow
New powers and nobler duties than you know.
Rise to the thought ! Live in the widening race !
Help make the State more like God's dwelling-
    place !
New paths for life divine, as yet untrod, —
A social body for the soul of God !

HOW WOULD YOU ?

HALF of our misery, half our pain,
Half the dark background of our self-reproach,
Is thought of how the world has sinned before.
We, being one, one with all life, we feel

The misdemeanors of uncounted time;
We suffer in the foolishness and sins
Of races just behind us, — burn with shame
At their gross ignorance and murderous deeds ;
We suffer back of them in the long years
Of squalid struggling savagery of beasts, —
Beasts human and subhuman; back of them
In helpless creatures eaten, hunted, torn ;
In submerged forests dying in the slime ;
And even back of that in endless years
Of hot convulsions of dismembered lands,
And slow constricting centuries of cold.
So in our own lives, even to this day,
We carry in the chambers of the mind
The tale of errors, failures, and misdeeds
That we call sins, of all our early lives.
And the recurrent consciousness of this
We call remorse. The unrelenting gauge,
Now measuring past error, — this is shame.
And in our feverish overconsciousness,
A retroactive and preactive sense, —
Fired with our self-made theories of sin, —
We suffer, suffer, suffer — half alive,
And half with the dead scars of suffering.

Friends, how would you, perhaps, have made
    the world?
Would you have balanced the great forces so

Their interaction would have bred no shock?
No cosmic throes of newborn continents,
No eras of the earth-encircling rain, —
Uncounted scalding tears that fell and fell
On molten worlds that hotly dashed them back
In storms of fierce repudiated steam?
Would you have made earth's gems without the
    fire,
Without the water, and without the weight
Of crushing cubic miles of huddled rock?
Would you have made one kind of plant to reign
In all the earth, growing mast high, and then
Keep it undying so, an end of plants?
Would you have made one kind of animal
To live on air and spare the tender grass,
And stop him, somehow, when he grew so thick
That even air fell short. Or would you have
All plants and animals, and make them change
By some metempsychosis not called death?
For, having them, you have to have them change,
For growth is change, and life is growth; and change
Implies — in this world — what we miscall pain.

You, wiser, would have made mankind, no doubt,
Not slowly, awfully, from dying brutes
Up into living humanness at last,
But fresh as Adam in the Hebrew tale;
Only you would have left the serpent out,

And left him, naked, in the garden still.
Or somehow, dodging this, have still contrived
That he should learn the whole curriculum
And never miss a lesson — never fail —
Be born, like Buddha, all accomplished, wise.
Would you have chosen to begin life old,
Well-balanced, cautious, knowing where to step,
And so untortured by the memory
Of childhood's foolishness and youth's mistakes?
Or, born a child, to have experience
Come to you softly without chance of loss,
Recurring years each rolling to your hand
In blissful innocent unconsciousness?

O dreamers with a Heaven and a Hell
Standing at either end of your wild rush
Away from the large peace of knowing God,
Can you not see that all of it is good?
Good, with the postulate that this is life, —
And that is all we have to argue from.
Childhood means error, the mistakes that teach ;
But only rod and threat and nurse's tale,
Make childhood's errors bring us shame and sin.
The race's childhood grows by error too,
And we are not attained to manhood yet.
But grief and shame are only born of lies.
Once see the lovely law that needs mistakes,
And you are young forever.   This is Life.

A MAN MUST LIVE.

A MAN must live. We justify
Low shift and trick to treason high,
　A little vote for a little gold
　To a whole senate bought and sold,
By that self-evident reply.

But is it so? Pray tell me why
Life at such cost you have to buy?
　In what religion were you told
　　A man must live?

There are times when a man must die.
Imagine, for a battle-cry,
　From soldiers, with a sword to hold, —
　From soldiers, with the flag unrolled, —
This coward's whine, this liar's lie, —
　　A man must live !

IN DUTY BOUND.

IN duty bound, a life hemmed in
　Whichever way the spirit turns to look;
No chance of breaking out, except by sin;
　　Not even room to shirk —
　　Simply to live, and work.

An obligation pre-imposed, unsought,
  Yet binding with the force of natural law;
The pressure of antagonistic thought ;
    Aching within, each hour,
    A sense of wasting power.

A house with roof so darkly low
  The heavy rafters shut the sunlight out;
One cannot stand erect without a blow ;
    Until the soul inside
    Cries for a grave — more wide.

A consciousness that if this thing endure,
  The common joys of life will dull the pain;
The high ideals of the grand and pure
    Die, as of course they must,
    Of long disuse and rust.

That is the worst. It takes supernal strength
  To hold the attitude that brings the pain ;
And they are few indeed but stoop at length
    To something less than best,
    To find, in stooping, rest.

DESIRE.

Lo, I desire! Sum of the ages' growth —
Fruit of evolving eras — king of life —
I, holding in myself the outgrown past
In all its ever-rising forms — desire.

THE WORLD.

With the first grass-blade, I desire the sun;
With every bird that breathes, I love the air;
With fishes, joy in water; with my horse,
Exult in motion; with all living flesh,
Long for sweet food and warmth and mate and
    young;
With the whole rising tide of that which is,
Thirst for advancement, — crave and yearn for it!
Yea, I desire! Then the compelling will
Urges to action to attain desire.
What action? Which desire? Am I a plant,
Rooted and helpless, following the light
Without volition? Or am I a beast,
Led by desire into the hunter's snare?
Am I a savage, swayed by every wish,
Brutal and feeble, a ferocious child?
Stand back, Desire, and put your plea in words.
No wordless wailing for the summer moon,
No Gilpin race on some strong appetite,
Stand here before the King, and make your plea.
If Reason sees it just, you have your wish;
If not, your wish is vain, plead as you will.
The court is open, beggar! I am King!

WHY NOT?

WHY not look forward far as Plato looked
And see the beauty of our coming life,

35

As he saw that which might be ours to-day?
If his soul, then, could rise so far beyond
The brutal average of that old time,
When icy peaks of art stood sheer and high
In fat black valleys where the helot toiled ;
If he, from that, could see so far ahead,
Could forecast days when Love and Justice both
Should watch the cradle of a healthy child,
And Wisdom walk with Beauty and pure Joy
In all the common ways of daily life, —
Then may not we, from great heights hardly won,
Bright hills of liberty, broad plains of peace,
And flower-sweet valleys of warm human love,
Still broken by the chasms of despair
Where Poverty and Ignorance and Sin
Pollute the air of all, — why not, from this,
Look on as Plato looked, and see the day
When his Republic and our Heaven, joined,
Shall make life what God meant it?
                    Ay, we do!

OUT OF THE GATE.

Out of the glorious city gate
A great throng came.
A mighty throng that swelled and grew
Around a face that all men knew —

A man who bore a noted name —
Gathered to listen to his fate.

The Judge sat high. Unbroken black
Around, above, and at his back.
The people pressed for nearer place,
Longing, yet shamed, to watch that face;
And in a space before the throne
The prisoner stood, unbound, alone.
So thick they rose on every side,
There was no spot his face to hide.

Then came the Herald, crying clear,
That all the listening crowd should hear;
Crying aloud before the sun
What thing this fallen man had done.
He — who had held a ruler's place
Among them, by their choice and grace —
He — fallen lower than the dust —
Had sinned against his public trust!

The Herald ceased. The Poet arose,
The Poet, whose awful art now shows
To this poor heart, and heart of every one,
The horror of the thing that he had done.

"O Citizen! Dweller in this high place!
Son of the city! Sharer in its pride!
Born in the light of its fair face!

By it fed, sheltered, taught, and glorified!
Raised to pure manhood by thy city's care;
Made strong and beautiful and happy there;
Loving thy mother and thy father more
For the fair town which made them glad before;
Finding among its maidens thy sweet wife;
Owing to it thy power and place in life;
Raised by its people to the lofty stand
Where thou couldst execute their high com-
    mand;
Trusted and honored, lifted over all, —
So honored and so trusted, didst thou fall!
Against the people — who gave thee the power —
Thou hast misused it in an evil hour!
Against the city where thou owest all —
Thy city, man, within whose guarding wall
Lie all our life's young glories — ay, the whole!
The home and cradle of the human soul!
Against thy city, beautiful and strong,
Thou, with the power it gave, hast done this
    wrong!"

Then rose the Judge. "Prisoner, thy case was tried
Fairly and fully in the courts inside.
Thy guilt was proven, and thou hast confessed,
And now the people's voice must do the rest.
I speak the sentence which the people give:
It is permitted thee to freely live,

Redeem thy sin by service to the state,
But nevermore within this city's gate ! "

Back rolled the long procession, sad and slow,
Back where the city's thousand banners blow.
The solemn music rises glad and clear
When the great gates before them open near,
Rises in triumph, sinks to sweet repose,
When the great gates behind them swing and close.
Free stands the prisoner, with a heart of stone.
The city gate is shut. He is alone.

THE MODERN SKELETON.

As kings of old in riotous royal feasts,
Among the piled up roses and the wine,
Wild music and soft-footed dancing girls,
The pearls and gold and barbarous luxury,
Used to show also a white skeleton, —
To make life meeker in the sight of death,
To make joy sweeter by the thought thereof, —

So our new kings in their high banqueting,
With the electric lustre unforeseen,
And unimagined costliness of flowers;
Rich wines of price and food as rare as gems,
And all the wondrous waste of artifice;
Midst high-bred elegance and jewelled ease

And beauty of rich raiment; they should set,
High before all, a sickly pauper child,
To keep the rich in mind of poverty, —
The sure concomitant of their estate.

THE LESSON OF DEATH.

TO S. T. D.

In memory of one whose breath
Blessed all with words wise, loving, brave;
Whose life was service, and whose death
Unites our hearts around her grave.

. . . .

Another blow has fallen, Lord —
         Was it from thee?
Is it indeed thy fiery sword
That cuts our hearts ?   We know thy word;
We know by heart wherein it saith
" Whom the Lord loves he chasteneth " —
But also, in another breath,
This : " The wages of sin is death."

How may we tell what pain is good,
         In mercy sent ?
And what is evil through and through,
Sure consequence of what we do,
Sure product of thy broken laws,
Certain effect of given cause,
         Just punishment ?

THE WORLD.

Not sin of those who suffer, Lord —
   To them no shame.
For father's sins our children die
With Justice sitting idly by;
The guilty thrive nor yet repent,
While sorrow strikes the innocent —
   Whom shall we blame?

'T is not that one alone is dead,
   And these bereft.
For her, for them, we grieve indeed;
But there are other hearts that bleed!
All up and down the world so wide
We suffer, Lord, on every side, —
   We who are left.

See now, we bend our stricken hearts,
   Patient and still,
Knowing thy laws are wholly just,
Knowing thy love commands our trust,
Knowing that good is God alone,
That pain and sorrow are our own,
And seeking out of all our pain
To struggle up to God again —
   Teach us thy will!

When shall we learn by common joy
   Broad as the sun,
By common effort, common fear,
All common life that holds us near,

41

And this great bitter common pain
Coming again and yet again —
        That we are one?

Yea, one. We cannot sin apart,
        Suffer alone ;
Nor keep our goodness to ourselves
Like precious things on hidden shelves.
Because we each live not our best,
Some one must suffer for the rest —
        For we are one !

Our pain is but the voice of wrong —
        Lord, help us hear !
Teach us to see the truth at last,
To mend our future from our past,
To know thy laws and find them friends,
Leading us safe to lovely ends,
        Thine own hand near.

Not one by doing right alone
        Can mend the way;
But we must all do right together, —
Love, help, and serve each other, whether
We joy or suffer. So at last
Shall needless pain and death be past,
And we, thy children living here,
Be worthy of our father dear !
        God speed the day !
  ·   ·   ·   ·   ·   ·   ·   ·

Oh, help us, Father, from this loss
        To learn thy will!
So shall our lost one live again;
So shall her life not pass in vain;
So shall we show in better living —
In loving, helping, doing, giving —
        That she lives still!

FOR US.

If we have not learned that God 's in man,
        And man in God again;
That to love thy God is to love thy brother,
And to serve the Lord is to serve each other, —
        Then Christ was born in vain!

If we have not learned that one man's life
        In all men lives again;
That each man's battle, fought alone,
Is won or lost for every one, —
        Then Christ hath lived in vain!

If we have not learned that death 's no break
        In life's unceasing chain;
That the work in one life well begun
In others is finished, by others is done, —
        Then Christ hath died in vain!

43

If we have not learned of immortal life,
 And a future free from pain;
The kingdom of God in the heart of man,
And the living world on Heaven's plan, —
 Then Christ arose in vain!

THANKSGIVING.

WELL is it for the land whose people, yearly,
 Turn to the Giver of all Good with praise,
Chanting glad hymns that thank him, loudly,
 clearly,
 Rejoicing in the beauty of his ways.

Great name that means all perfectness and power!
 We thank thee — not for mercy, nor release,
But for clear joy in sky and sea and flower,
 In thy pure justice, and thy blessed peace.

We live; behind us the dark past; before,
 A wide way full of light that thou dost give;
More light, more strength, more joy and ever
 more —
 O God of joy! we thank thee that we live!

CHRISTMAS HYMN.

LISTEN not to the word that would have you believe
That the voice of the age is a moan;

44

THE WORLD.

That the red hand of wrong
Is triumphant and strong,
And that wrong is triumphant alone;
There was never a time on the face of the earth
When love was so near its own.

Do you think that the love which has died for the
world
Has not lived for the world also?
Filling man with the fire
Of a boundless desire
To love all with a love that shall grow?
It was not for nothing the White Christ was born
Two thousand years ago.

The power that gave birth to the Son of the King
All life doth move and thrill,
Every age as 't is passed
Coming nearer at last
To the law of that wonderful will, —
As our God so loved the world that day,
Our God so loves it still.

The love that fed poverty, making it thrive,
Is learning a lovelier way.
We have seen that the poor
Need be with us no more,
And that sin may be driven away;
The love that has carried the martyrs to death
Is entering life to-day.

The spirit of Christ is awake and alive,
In the work of the world it is shown,
Crying loud, crying clear,
That the Kingdom is here,
And that all men are heirs to the throne!
There was never a time since the making of man
When love was so near its own!

CHRISTMAS.

Slow, slow and weak,
As first the tongue began to speak,
The hand to serve, the heart to feel,
Grew up among our mutual deeds,
Great flower out-topping all the weeds,
Sweet fruit that meets all human needs,
Our love — our common weal.

It spread so wide, so high,
We saw it broad against the sky,
Down shining where we trod ;
It stormed our new-born consciousness,
Omnipotent to heal and bless,
Till we conceived — we could no less,
It was the love of God!

Came there a man at length
Whose heart so swelled with the great strength
Of love that would have way,

46

That in his body he fulfilled
The utmost service love had willed;
And the great stream, so held, so spilled,
    Pours on until to-day.

Still we look back to this grand dream,
Still stoop to drink at this wide stream,
Wider each year we live;   '
And on one yearly blessed day,
Seek not to earn and not to pay,
But to let love have its one way, —
    To quench our thirst *to give !*

Brothers, cease not to bless the name
Of him who loved through death and shame,
We cannot praise amiss;
But not in vain was sown the seed;
Look wide where thousands toil and bleed,
Where men meet death for common need —
    Hath no man loved but this?

Yea, all men love; we love to-day
Wide as the human race has sway,
Ever more deep, more dear;
No stream, — an everlasting sea,
Beating and throbbing to be free,
To give it forth there needs must be
    One Christmas all the year!

THE LIVING GOD.

THE Living God.   The God that made the world
Made it, and stood aside to watch and wait,
Arranging a predestined plan
To save the erring soul of man —
Undying destiny — unswerving fate.
I see his hand in the path of life,   \
His law to doom and save,
His love divine in the hopes that shine
Beyond the sinner's grave,
His care that sendeth sun and rain,
His wisdom giving rest,
His price of sin that we may not win
The heaven of the blest.

> Not near enough !   Not clear enough !
>   O God, come nearer still !
> I long for thee !   Be strong for me !
>   Teach me to know thy will !

The Living God.   The God that makes the world,
Makes it — is making it in all its worth ;
His spirit speaking sure and slow
In the real universe we know, —
God living in the earth.
I feel his breath in the blowing wind,
His pulse in the swinging sea,
And the sunlit sod is the breast of God

Whose strength we feel and see.
His tenderness in the springing grass,
His beauty in the flowers,
His living love in the sun above, —
All here, and near, and ours !

Not near enough ! Not clear enough !
O God, come nearer still !
I long for thee ! Be strong for me !
Teach me to know thy will !

The Living God. The God that is the world.
The world? The world is man, — the work of man.
Then — dare I follow what I see ? —
Then — by thy Glory — it must be
That we are in thy plan ?
That strength divine in the work we do ?
That love in our mothers' eyes ?
That wisdom clear in our thinking here ?
That power to help us rise ?
God in the daily work we 've done,
In the daily path we 've trod ?
Stand still, my heart, for I am a part —
I too — of the Living God !

Ah, clear as light ! As near ! As bright !
O God ! My God ! My Own !
Command thou me ! I stand for thee !
And I do not stand alone !

A PRAYER.

O GOD! I cannot ask thee to forgive;
　　I have done wrong.
Thy law is just; thy law must live, —
Whoso doth wrong must suffer pain.
But help me to do right again, —
　　Again be strong.

GIVE WAY!

SHALL we not open the human heart,
Swing the doors till the hinges start;
　　Stop our worrying doubt and din,
　　Hunting heaven and dodging sin?
There is no need to search so wide,
Open the door and stand aside —
　　Let God in!

Shall we not open the human heart
To loving labor in field and mart;
　　Working together for all about,
　　The glad, large labor that knows not doubt?
Can He be held in our narrow rim?
Do the work that is work for Him —
　　Let God out!

Shall we not open the human heart,
Never to close and stand apart?

THE WORLD.

God is a force to give way to!
God is a thing you have to do!
God can never be caught by prayer,
Hid in your heart and fastened there —
Let God through!

THANKSGIVING HYMN.

FOR CALIFORNIA.

Our forefathers gave thanks to God,
In the land by the stormy sea,
For bread hard wrung from the iron sod
In cold and misery.
Though every day meant toil and strife,
In the land by the stormy sea,
They thanked their God for the gift of life —
How much the more should we!

Stern frost had they full many a day,
Strong ice on the stormy sea,
Long months of snow, gray clouds hung low,
And a cold wind endlessly;
Winter, and war with an alien race —
But they were alive and free!
And they thanked their God for his good grace —
How much the more should we!

For we have a land all sunny with gold, —
A land by the summer sea;

Gold in the earth for our hands to hold,
  Gold in blossom and tree;
Comfort, and plenty, and beauty, and peace,
  From the mountains down to the sea.
They thanked their God for a year's increase —
  How much the more should we !

CHRISTMAS CAROL.

FOR LOS ANGELES.

On the beautiful birthday of Jesus,
  While the nations praising stand,
He goeth from city to city,
  He walketh from land to land.

And the snow lies white and heavy,
  And the ice lies wide and wan,
But the love of the blessed Christmas
  Melts even the heart of man.

With love from the heart of Heaven,
  In the power of his Holy Name,
To the City of the Queen of the Angels
  The tender Christ-child came.

The land blushed red with roses,
  The land laughed glad with grain,
And the little hills smiled softly
  In the freshness after rain.

THE WORLD.

Land of the fig and olive!
  Land of the fruitful vine!
His heart grew soft within him,
  As he thought of Palestine, –

Of the brooks with the banks of lilies,
  Of the little doves of clay,
And of how he sat with his mother
  At the end of a summer's day,

His head on his mother's bosom,
  His hand in his mother's hand,
Watching the golden sun go down
  Across the shadowy land, –

A moment's life with human kind;
  A moment, — nothing more;
Eternity lies broad behind,
  Eternity before.

High on the Hills of Heaven,
  Majestic, undefiled,
Forever and ever he lives, a God;
  But once he lived, a Child!

And the child-heart leaps within him,
  And the child-eyes softer grow,
When the land lies bright and sunny,
  Like the land of long ago;

And the love of God is mingled
With the love of dear days gone,
When he comes to the city of his mother,
On the day her child was born!

NEW DUTY.

ONCE to God we owed it all, —
God alone;
Bowing in eternal thrall,
Giving, sacrificing all,
Before the Throne.

Once we owed it to the King, —
Served the crown;
Life, and love, and everything,
In allegiance to the King,
Laying down.

Now we owe it to Mankind, —
To our Race;
Fullest fruit of soul and mind,
Heart and hand and all behind,
Now in place.

Loving-service, wide and free,
From the sod
Up in varying degree,
Through me and you — through you and me —
Up to God!

SEEKING.

I WENT to look for Love among the roses, the roses,
The pretty wingèd boy with the arrow and the bow;
    In the fair and fragrant places,
    'Mid the Muses and the Graces,
At the feet of Aphrodite, with the roses all aglow.

Then I sought among the shrines where the rosy
    flames were leaping —
The rose and golden flames, never ceasing, never
    still —
    For the boy so fair and slender,
    The imperious, the tender,
With the whole world moving slowly to the music
    of his will.

Sought, and found not for my seeking, till the sweet
    quest led me further,
And before me rose the temple, marble-based and
    gold above,
    Where the long procession marches
    'Neath the incense-clouded arches
In the world-compelling worship of the mighty God
    of Love.

Yea, I passed with bated breath to the holiest of
    holies,
And I lifted the great curtain from the Inmost, —
    the Most Fair, —

Eager for the joy of finding,
For the glory, beating, blinding,
Meeting but an empty darkness; darkness, silence
— nothing there.

Where is Love? I cried in anguish, while the
  temple reeled and faded ;
Where is Love? — for I must find him, I must
  know and understand !
Died the music and the laughter,
Flames and roses dying after,
And the curtain I was holding fell to ashes in my
  hand.

FINDING.

OUT of great darkness and wide wastes of silence,
  Long loneliness, and slow untasted years,
Came a slow filling of the empty places,
A slow, sweet lighting of forgotten faces,
  A smiling under tears.

A light of dawn that filled the brooding heaven,
  A warmth that kindled all the earth and air,
A thrilling tender music, floating, stealing,
A fragrance of unnumbered flowers revealing
  A sweetness new and fair.

After the loss of love where I had sought him,
  After the anguish of the empty shrine,

Came a warm joy from all the hearts around me,
A feeling that some perfect strength had found
   me,
      Touch of the hand divine.

I followed Love to his intensest centre,
   And lost him utterly when fastened there;
I let him go and ceased my selfish seeking,
Turning my heart to all earth's voices speaking,
    And found him everywhere.

Love like the rain that falls on just and unjust,
   Love like the sunshine, measureless and free,
From each to all, from all to each, to live in;
And, in the world's glad love so gladly given,
    Came heart's true love to me!

TOO MUCH.

THERE are who die without love, never seeing
The clear eyes shining, the bright wings fleeing.
Lonely they die, and ahungered, in bitterness
   knowing
They have not had their share of the good there
   was going.

There are who have and lose love, these most
   blessed,
In joy unstained which they have once possessed,

Lost while still dear, still sweet, still met by glad
    affection, —
An endless happiness in recollection.

And some have Love 's full cup as he doth give it —
Have it, and drink of it, and, ah, — outlive it !
Full fed by Love 's delights, o'erwearied, sated,
They die, not hungry — only suffocated.

THE CUP.

AND yet, saith he, ye need but sip;
    And who would die without a taste?
Just touch the goblet to the lip,
    Then let the bright draught run to waste !

She set her lip to the beaker's brim —
    'T was passing sweet ! 'T was passing mild !
She let her large eyes dwell on him,
    And sipped again, and smiled.

So sweet ! So mild ! She scarce can tell
    If she doth really drink or no ;
Till the light doth fade and the shadows swell,
    And the goblet lieth low.

O cup of dreams ! O cup of doubt !
    O cup of blinding joy and pain !
The taste that none would die without !
    The draught that all the world must drain !

WHAT THEN?

SUPPOSE you write your heart out till the world
    Sobs with one voice — what then?
Small agonies that round your heart-strings curled
    Strung out for choice, that men
May pick a phrase, each for his own pet pain,
      And thank the voice so come,
      They being dumb. What then?

You have no sympathy? O endless claim!
    No one that cares? What then?
Suppose you had — the whole world knew your
      name
    And your affairs, and men
Ached with your headache, dreamed your dreadful
      dreams,
      And, with your heart-break due,
      Their hearts broke too. What then?

You think that people do not understand?
    You suffer? Die? What then?
Unhappy child, look here, on either hand,
    Look low or high, — all men
Suffer and die, and keep it to themselves!
      They die— they suffer sore —
      You suffer more? What then?

OUR LONELINESS.

THERE is no deeper grief than loneliness.
Our sharpest anguish at the death of friends
Is loneliness. Our agony of heart
When love has gone from us is loneliness.
The crying of a little child at night
In the big dark is crowding loneliness.
Slow death of woman on a Kansas farm;
The ache of those who think beyond their time;
Pain unassuaged of isolated lives, —
All this is loneliness.

Oh, we who are one body of one soul!
Great soul of man born into social form!
Should we not suffer at dismemberment?
A finger torn from brotherhood; an eye
Having no cause to see when set alone.
Our separation is the agony
Of uses unfulfilled — of thwarted law;
The forces of all nature throb and push,
Crying for their accustomed avenues;
And we, alone, have no excuse to be, —
No reason for our being. We are dead
Before we die, and know it in our hearts.

Even the narrowest union has some joy,
Transient and shallow, limited and weak;
And joy of union strengthens with its strength,

Deepens and widens as the union grows.
Hence the pure light of long-enduring love,
Lives blended slowly, softly, into one.
Hence civic pride, and glory in our states,
And the fierce thrill of patriotic fire
When millions feel as one!

                       When we shall learn
To live together fully ; when each man
And woman works in conscious interchange
With all the world, — union as wide as man, —
No human soul can ever suffer more
The devastating grief of loneliness.

THE KEEPER OF THE LIGHT.

A LIGHTHOUSE keeper with a loving heart
  Toiled at his service in the lonely tower,
Keeping his giant lenses clear and bright,
And feeding with pure oil the precious light
  Whose power to save was as his own heart's
  power.

He loved his kind, and being set alone
  To help them by the means of this great light,
He poured his whole heart's service into it,
And sent his love down the long beams that lit
  The waste of broken water in the night.

He loved his kind, and joyed to see the ships
  Come out of nowhere into his bright field,
And glide by safely with their living men,
Past him and out into the dark again,
  To other hands their freight of joy to yield.

His work was noble and his work was done ;
  He kept the ships in safety and was glad ;
And yet, late coming with the light's supplies,
They found the love no longer in his eyes —
  The keeper of the light had fallen mad.

IMMORTALITY.

WHEN I was grass, perhaps I may have wept
As every year the grass-blades paled and slept ;
Or shrieked in anguish impotent, beneath
The smooth impartial cropping of great teeth —
I don't remember much what came to pass
      When I was grass.

When I was monkey, I 'm afraid the trees
Were n't always havens of contented ease ;
Things killed us, and we never could tell why ;
No doubt we blamed the earth or sea or sky —
I have forgotten my rebellion's shape
      When I was ape.

Now I have reached the comfortable skin
This stage of living is enveloped in,
And hold the spirit of my mighty race
Self-conscious prisoner under one white face, —·
I 'm awfully afraid I 'm going to die,
      Now I am I.

So I have planned a hypothetic life
To pay me somehow for my toil and strife.
Blessed or damned, I someway must contrive
That I eternally be kept alive !
In this an endless, boundless bliss I see, —
      Eternal me !

.   .   .   .

When I was man, no doubt I used to care
About the little things that happened there,
And fret to see the years keep going by,
And nations, families, and persons die.
I did n't much appreciate life's plan
      When I was man.

WASTE.

Doth any man consider what we waste
Here in God's garden? While the sea is full,
The sunlight smiles, and all the blessed earth
Offers her wealth to our intelligence.
We waste our food, enough for half the world,

In helpless luxury among the rich,
In helpless ignorance among the poor,
In spilling what we stop to quarrel for.
We waste our wealth in failing to produce,
In robbing of each other every day
In place of making things, — our human crown.
We waste our strength, in endless effort poured
Like water on the sand, still toiling on
To make a million things we do not want.
We waste our lives, those which should still lead on,
Each new one gaining on the age behind,
In doing what we all have done before.
We waste our love, — poured up into the sky,
Across the ocean, into desert lands,
Sunk in one narrow circle next ourselves, —
While these, our brothers, suffer — are alone.
Ye may not pass the near to love the far ;
Ye may not love the near and stop at that.
Love spreads through man, not over or around !
Yea, grievously we waste ; and all the time
Humanity is wanting, — wanting sore.
Waste not, my brothers, and ye shall not want !

WINGS.

A sense of wings —
  Soft downy wings and fair —
Great wings that whistle as they sweep

Along the still gulfs — empty, deep —
Of thin blue air.

Doves' wings that follow,
　Doves' wings that fold,
Doves' wings that flutter down
　To nestle in your hold.

Doves' wings that settle,
　Doves' wings that rest,
Doves' wings that brood so warm
　Above the little nest.

Larks' wings that rise and rise,
Climbing the rosy skies —
　　Fold and drop down
　　To birdlings brown.

Light wings of wood-birds, that one scarce believes
　Moved in the leaves.

　The quick, shy flight
　Of wings that flee in fright —
　A start as swift as light —
　Only the shaken air
　To tell that wings were there.

Broad wings that beat for many days
Above the land wastes and the water ways;
　Beating steadily on and on,

Through dark and cold,
Through storms untold,
Till the far sun and summer land is won.

And wings —
Wings that unfold
With such wide sweep before your would-be hold —
Such glittering sweep of whiteness — sun on
snow —
Such mighty plumes — strong-ribbed, strong-
webbed — strong-knit to go
From earth to heaven !
Hear the air flow back
In their wide track !
Feel the sweet wind these wings displace
Beat on your face !
See the great arc of light like rising rockets trail
They leave in leaving —
They avail —
These wings — for flight !

THE HEART OF THE WATER.

O THE ache in the heart of the water that lies
Underground in the desert, unopened, unknown,
While the seeds lie unbroken, the blossoms un-
blown,
And the traveller wanders — the traveller dies !

O the joy in the heart of the water that flows
From the well in the desert, — a desert no more, —
Bird-music and blossoms and harvest in store,
And the white shrine that showeth the traveller
    knows !

THE SHIP.

THE sunlight is mine !   And the sea !
    And the four wild winds that blow !
The winds of heaven that whistle free —
They are but slaves to carry me
        Wherever I choose to go !

Fire for a power inside !
    Air for a pathway free !
I traverse the earth in conquest wide;
The sea is my servant !   The sea is my bride !
    And the elements wait on me !
    .   .   .   .

In dull green light, down-filtered sick and slow
Through miles of heavy water overhead,
With miles of heavy water yet below,
        A ship lies, dead.
Shapeless and broken, swayed from side to side,
The helpless driftwood of an unknown tide.

AMONG THE GODS.

How close the air of valleys, and how close
The teeming little life that harbors there !

For me, I will climb mountains. Up and up,
Higher and higher, till I pant for breath
In that thin clearness. Still? There is no sound
Nor memory of sound upon these heights.
Ah! the great sunlight! The caressing sky,
The beauty, and the stillness, and the peace!
I see my pathway clear for miles below;
See where I fell, and set a friendly sign
To warn some other of the danger there.
The green small world is wide below me spread.
The great small world! Some things look large
    and fair
Which, in their midst, I could not even see;
And some look small which used to terrify.
Blessed these heights of freedom, wisdom, rest!
I will go higher yet.

        A sea of cloud
Rolls soundless waves between me and the world.
This is the zone of everlasting snows,
And the sweet silence of the hills below
Is song and laughter to the silence here.
Great fields, huge peaks, long awful slopes of snow.
Alone, triumphant, man above the world,
I stand among these white eternities.

        Sheer at my feet
Sink the unsounded, cloud-encumbered gulfs;
And shifting mists now veil and now reveal

The unknown fastnesses above me yet.
I am alone — above all life — sole king
Of these white wastes. How pitiful and small
Becomes the outgrown world! I reign supreme,
And in this utter stillness and wide peace
Look calmly down upon the universe.

Surely that crest has changed! That pile of cloud
That covers half the sky, waves like a robe!
                That large and gentle wind
Is like the passing of a presence here!
See how yon massive mist-enshrouded peak
Is like the shape of an unmeasured foot, —
The figure with the stars!
Ah! what is this? It moves, lifts, bends, is gone!

With what a shocking sense of littleness —
A reeling universe that changes place,
And falls to new relation over me —
I feel the unseen presence of the gods!

SONGS.

I.

O WORLD of green, all shining, shifting!
O world of blue, all living, lifting!
O world where glassy waters smoothly roll!

IN THIS OUR WORLD.

Fair earth, and heaven free,
Ye are but part of me —
Ye are my soul!

O woman nature, shining, shifting!
O woman creature, living, lifting!
Come soft and still to one who waits thee here!
Fair soul, both mine and free,
Ye who are part of me,
Appear! Appear!

II.

How could I choose but weep?
The poor bird lay asleep;
For lack of food, for lack of breath,
For lack of life he came to death —
How could I choose but weep?

How could I choose but smile?
There was no lack the while!
In bliss he did undo himself;
Where life was full he slew himself —
How could I choose but smile?

Would ye but understand!
Joy is on every hand!
Ye shut your eyes and call it night,
Ye grope and fall in seas of light —
Would ye but understand!

HEAVEN.

THOU bright mirage, that o'er man's arduous way
  Hast hung in the hot sky, with fountains stream-
    ing,
  Cool marble domes, and palm-fronds waving,
    gleaming, —
Vision of rest and peace to end the day !
Now he is weariest, alone, astray,
  Spent with long labor, led by thy sweet seem-
    ing,
  Faint as the breath of Nature's lightest dreaming,
Thou waverest and vanishest away !

Can Nature dream?   Is God's great sky deceiving?
  Where joy like that the clouds above us show
  Be sure the counterpart must lie below,
Sweeter than hope, more blessed than believing !
  We lose the fair reflection of our home
  Because so near its gates our feet have come !

BALLAD OF THE SUMMER SUN.

IT is said that human nature needeth hardship to
    be strong,
That highest growth has come to man in countries
    white with snow ;
And they tell of truth and wisdom that to north-
    ern folk belong,

71

And claim the brain is feeble where the south
    winds always blow.
They forget to read the story of the ages long ago:
The lore that built the pyramids where still the
    simoom veers,
The knowledge framing Tyrian ships, the greater
    skill that steers,
The learning of the Hindu in his volumes never
    done;
All the wisdom of Egyptians and the old Chaldean
    seers, —
Came to man in summer lands beneath a summer
    sun.

It is said that human nature needeth hardship to
    be strong,
That courage bred of meeting cold makes martial
    bosoms glow ;
And they point to mighty generals the northern
    folk among,
And call mankind emasculate where southern waters
    flow.
They forget to look at history and see the nations
    grow !
The cohorts of Assyrian kings, the Pharaohs' char-
    ioteers,
The march of Alexander, the Persians' conquering
    spears,

The legions of the Romans, from Ethiop to Hun,
The power that mastered all the world and held it
    years on years, —
Came to man in summer lands beneath a summer
    sun.

It is said that human nature needeth hardship to
    be strong,
That only pain and suffering the power to feel
    bestow;
And they show us noble artists made great by loss
    and wrong,
And say the soul is lowered that hath pleasure
    without woe.
They forget the perfect monuments that pleasure's
    blessings show;
The statue and the temple that no man living nears,
Song and verse and music forever in the ears,
The glory that remaineth while the sands of time
    shall run,
The beauty of immortal art that never disappears, —
Came to man in summer lands beneath a summer
    sun.

The faith of Thor and Odin, the creed of force
    and fears,
Cruel gods that deal in death, the icebound soul
    reveres,

But the Lord of Peace and Blessing was not one !
Truth and Power and Beauty — Love that endeth
    tears —
Came to man in summer lands beneath a summer
    sun.

PIONEERS.

LONG have we sung our noble pioneers,
    Vanguard of progress, heralds of the time,
    Guardians of industry and art sublime,
Leaders of man down all the brightening years!
To them the danger, to their wives the tears,
    While we sit safely in the city's grime,
    In old-world trammels of distress and crime,
Playing with words and thoughts, with doubts and
    fears.

Children of axe and gun!   Ye take to-day
    The baby steps of man's first, feeblest age,
    While we, thought-seekers of the printed page,
We lead the world down its untrodden way!
    Ours the drear wastes and leagues of empty waves,
    The lonely deaths, the undiscovered graves.

EXILES.

EXILED from home.   The far sea rolls
Between them and the country of their birth ;
The childhood-turning impulse of their souls
    Pulls half across the earth.

Exiled from home. No mother to take care
That they work not too hard, grieve not too sore;
No older brother nor small sister fair;
 No father any more.

Exiled from home; from all familiar things;
The low-browed roof, the grass-surrounded door;
Accustomed labors that gave daylight wings;
 Loved steps on the worn floor.

Exiled from home. Young girls sent forth alone
When most their hearts need close companioning;
No love and hardly friendship may they own,
 No voice of welcoming.

Blinded with homesick tears the exile stands;
To toil for alien household gods she comes;
A servant and a stranger in our lands,
 Homeless within our homes.

A NEVADA DESERT.

An aching, blinding, barren, endless plain,
 Corpse-colored with white mould of alkali,
Hairy with sage-brush, slimy after rain,
Burnt with the sky's hot scorn, and still again
 Sullenly burning back against the sky.

Dull green, dull brown, dull purple, and dull gray,
 The hard earth white with ages of despair,

Slow-crawling, turbid streams where dead reeds
 sway,
Low wall of sombre mountains far away,
 And sickly steam of geysers on the air.

TREE FEELINGS.

I WONDER if they like it — being trees?
I suppose they do. . , .
It must feel good to have the ground so flat,
And feel yourself stand right straight up like that —
So stiff in the middle — and then branch at ease,
Big boughs that arch, small ones that bend and
 blow,
And all those fringy leaves that flutter so.
You 'd think they 'd break off at the lower end
When the wind fills them, and their great heads
 bend.
But then you think of all the roots they drop,
As much at bottom as there is on top, —
A double tree, widespread in earth and air
Like a reflection in the water there.

I guess they like to stand still in the sun
And just breathe out and in, and feel the cool sap
 run ;
And like to feel the rain run through their hair
And slide down to the roots and settle there.

But I think they like wind best.   From the light
   touch
That lets the leaves whisper and kiss so much,
To the great swinging, tossing, flying wide,
And all the time so stiff and strong inside !
And the big winds, that pull, and make them feel
How long their roots are, and the earth how leal !

And O the blossoms !   And the wild seeds lost !
And jewelled martyrdom of fiery frost !
And fruit trees.   I 'd forgotten.   No cold gem,
But to be apples — and bow down with them !

MONOTONY.

FROM CALIFORNIA.

WHEN ragged lines of passing days go by,
Crowding and hurried, broken-linked and slow,
Some sobbing pitifully as they pass,
Some angry-hot and fierce, some angry cold,
Some raging and some wailing, and again
The fretful days one cannot read aright, —
Then truly, when the fair days smile on us,
We feel that loveliness with sharper touch
And grieve to lose it for the next day's chance.
And so men question — they who never know
If beauty comes or horror, pain or joy —
If we, whose sky is peace, whose hours are glad,
Find not our happiness monotonous !

But when the long procession of the days
Rolls musically down the waiting year,
Close-ranked, rich-robed, flower-garlanded and fair;
Broad brows of peace, deep eyes of soundless truth,
And lips of love, — warm, steady, changeless love;
Each one more beautiful, till we forget
Our niggard fear of losing half an hour,
And learn to count on more and ever more, —
In the remembered joy of yesterday,
In the full rapture of to-day's delight,
And knowledge of the happiness to come,
We learn to let life pass without regret,
We learn to hold life softly and in peace,
We learn to meet life gladly, full of faith,
We learn what God is, and to trust in Him !

THE BEDS OF FLEUR-DE-LYS.

HIGH-LYING, sea-blown stretches of green turf,
    Wind-bitten close, salt-colored by the sea,
Low curve on curve spread far to the cool sky,
And, curving over them as long they lie,
        Beds of wild fleur-de-lys.

Wide-flowing, self-sown, stealing near and far,
    Breaking the green like islands in the sea;
Great stretches at your feet, and spots that bend
Dwindling over the horizon's end, —
        Wild beds of fleur-de-lys.

The light keen wind streams on across the lifts,
  Thin wind of western springtime by the sea ;
The close turf smiles unmoved, but over her
Is the far-flying rustle and sweet stir
    In beds of fleur-de-lys.

And here and there across the smooth, low grass
  Tall maidens wander, thinking of the sea ;
And bend, and bend, with light robes blown aside,
For the blue lily-flowers that bloom so wide, —
    The beds of fleur-de-lys.

THE PRESIDIO, SAN FRANCISCO.

IT IS GOOD TO BE ALIVE.

IT is good to be alive when the trees shine green,
And the steep red hills stand up against the sky ;
Big sky, blue sky, with flying clouds between —
It is good to be alive and see the clouds drive by !

It is good to be alive when the strong winds blow,
The strong, sweet winds blowing straightly off the
    sea ;
Great sea, green sea, with swinging ebb and flow —
It is good to be alive and see the waves roll free !

THE CHANGELESS YEAR.

SOUTHERN CALIFORNIA.

Doth Autumn remind thee of sadness?
And Winter of wasting and pain?
Midsummer, of joy that was madness?
 Spring, of hope that was vain?

Do the Seasons fly fast at thy laughter?
Do the Seasons lag slow if thou weep,
Till thou long'st for the land lying after
 The River of Sleep?

Come here, where the West lieth golden
In the light of an infinite sun,
Where Summer doth Winter embolden
 Till they reign here as one !

Here the Seasons tread soft and steal slowly;
A moment of question and doubt —
Is it Winter? Come faster ! — come wholly ! —
 And Spring rusheth out !

We forget there are tempests and changes;
We forget there are days that are drear;
In a dream of delight, the soul ranges
 Through the measureless year.

Still the land is with blossoms enfolden,
Still the sky burneth blue in its deeps;
Time noddeth, 'mid poppies all golden,
 And memory sleeps.

WHERE MEMORY SLEEPS.

RONDEAU.

WHERE memory sleeps the soul doth rise,
Free of that past where sorrow lies,
    And storeth against future ills
    The courage of the constant hills,
The comfort of the quiet skies.

Fair is this land to tired eyes,
Where summer sunlight never dies,
    And summer's peace the spirit fills,
      Where memory sleeps.

Safe from the season's changing cries
And chill of yearly sacrifice,
    Great roses crowd the window-sills, —
    Calm roses that no winter kills.
The peaceful heart all pain denies,
      Where memory sleeps.

CALIFORNIA CAR WINDOWS.

LARK songs ringing to Heaven,
    Earth light clear as the sky ;
Air like the breath of a greenhouse
    With the greenhouse roof on high.

Flowers to see till you 're weary,
    To travel in hours and hours ;

Ranches of gold and purple,
  Counties covered with flowers!

A rainbow, a running rainbow,
  That flies at our side for hours;
A ribbon, a broidered ribbon,
  A rainbow ribbon of flowers.

LIMITS.

On sand — loose sand and shifting —
On sand — dry sand and drifting —
    The city grows to the west;
Not till its border reaches
The ocean-beaten beaches
      Will it rest.

On hills — steep hills and lonely,
That stop at cloudland only —
    The city climbs to the sky;
Not till the souls who make it
Touch the clear light and take it,
      Will it die.

POWELL STREET.

You start
From the town's hot heart
To ride up Powell Street.

Hotel and theatre and crowding shops,
And Market's cabled stream that never stops,
And the mixed hurrying beat
Of countless feet —
Take a front seat.
Before you rise
Six terraced hills, up to the low-hung skies;
Low where across the hill they seem to lie,
And then — how high !
Up you go slowly.   To the right
A wide square, green and bright.
Above that green a broad façade,
Strongly and beautifully made,
In warm clear color standeth fair and true
Against the blue.
Only, above, two purple domes rise bold,
Twin-budded spires, bright-tipped with balls of
      gold.
Past that, and up you glide,
Up, up, till, either side,
Wide earth and water stretch around — away —
The straits, the hills, and the low-lying, wide-spread,
      dusky bay.
Great houses here,
Dull, opulent, severe.
Dives' gold birds on guarding lamps a-wing —
Dead gold, that may not sing !
Fair on the other side

Smooth, steep-laid sweeps of turf and green boughs
 waving wide.
This is the hilltop's crown.
Below you, down
In blurred, dim streets, the market quarter lies,
Foul, narrow, torn with cries
Of tortured things in cages, and the smell
Of daily bloodshed rising ; that is hell.

But up here on the crown of Powell Street
The air is sweet ;
And the green swaying mass of eucalyptus bends
Like hands of friends,
To gladden you despite the mansions' frown.
Then you go down.

Down, down, and round the turns to lower grades ;
Lower in all ways ; darkening with the shades
Of poverty, old youth, and unearned age,
And that quick squalor which so blots the page
Of San Francisco's beauty, — swift decay
Chasing the shallow grandeur of a day.

Here, like a noble lady of lost state,
Still calmly smiling at encroaching fate,
Amidst the squalor, rises Russian Hill, —
Proud, isolated, lonely, lovely still.

So on you glide.
Till the blue straits lie wide

Before you; purple mountains loom across,
And islands green as moss;
With soft white fog-wreaths drifting, drifting
    through
To comfort you;
And light, low-singing waves that tell you reach
The end, — North Beach.

FROM RUSSIAN HILL.

A STRANGE day — bright and still;
Strange for the stillness here,
For the strong trade-winds blow
With such a steady sweep it seems like rest,
Forever steadily across the crest
    Of Russian Hill.

Still now and clear, —
So clear you count the houses spreading wide
In the fair cities on the farther side
Of our broad bay;
And brown Goat Island lieth large between,
Its brownness brightening into sudden green
    From rains of yesterday.

Blue? Blue above of Californian sky,
Which has no peer on earth for its pure flame;
Bright blue of bay and strait spread wide below,
And, past the low, dull hills that hem it so, —

Blue as the sky, blue as the placid bay, —
Blue mountains far away.

Thanks this year for the early rains that came
To bless us, meaning Summer by and by.
This is our Spring-in-Autumn, making one
The Indian Summer tenderness of sun —
Its hazy stillness, and soft far-heard sound —
And the sweet riot of abundant spring,
The greenness flaming out from everything,
      The sense of coming gladness in the ground.

From this high peace and purity look down;
Between you and the blueness lies the town.
Under those huddled roofs the heart of man
Beats warmer than this brooding day,
Spreads wider than the hill-rimmed bay,
And throbs to tenderer life, were it but seen,
      Than all this new-born, all-enfolding green!

Within that heart lives still
All that one guesses, dreams, and sees —
Sitting in sunlight, warm, at ease —
From this high island, — Russian Hill.

"AN UNUSUAL RAIN."

Again!
      Another day of rain!
      It has rained for years.

It never clears.
The clouds come down so low
They drag and drip
Across each hill-top's tip.
In progress slow
They blow in from the sea
Eternally;
Hang heavily and black,
And then roll back;
And rain and rain and rain,
Both drifting in and drifting out again.

They come down to the ground,
These clouds, where the ground is high;
And, lest the weather fiend forget
And leave one hidden spot unwet,
The fog comes up to the sky!
And all our pavement of planks and logs
Reeks with the rain and steeps in the fogs
Till the water rises and sinks and presses
Into your bonnets and shoes and dresses;
And every outdoor-going dunce
Is wet in forty ways at once.

Wet?
It 's wetter than being drowned.
Dark?
Such darkness never was found

Since first the light was made. And cold?
O come to the land of grapes and gold,
Of fruit and flowers and sunshine gay,
When the rainy season 's under way !

And they tell you calmly, evermore,
They never had such rain before !

What 's that you say ? Come out ?
Why, see that sky !
Oh, what a world ! so clear ! so high !
So clean and lovely all about ;
The sunlight burning through and through,
And everything just blazing blue.
And look ! the whole world blossoms again
The minute the sunshine follows the rain.
Warm sky — earth basking under —
Did it ever rain, I wonder ?

THE HILLS.

THE flowing waves of our warm sea
    Roll to the beach and die,
But the soul of the waves forever fills
The curving crests of our restless hills
    That climb so wantonly.

Up and up till you look to see
    Along the cloud-kissed top

The great hill-breakers curve and comb
In crumbling lines of falling foam
   Before they settle and drop.

Down and down, with the shuddering sweep
   Of the sea-wave's glassy wall,
You sink with a plunge that takes your breath,
A thrill that stirreth and quickeneth,
   Like the great line steamer's fall.

We have laid our streets by the square and line,
   We have built by the line and square;
But the strong hill-rises arch below
And force the houses to curve and flow
   In lines of beauty there.

And off to the north and east and south,
   With wildering mists between,
They ring us round with wavering hold,
With fold on fold of rose and gold,
   Violet, azure, and green.

CITY'S BEAUTY.

FAIR, oh, fair are the hills uncrowned,
   Only wreathed and garlanded
   With the soft clouds overhead,
With the waving streams of rain;
Fair in golden sunlight drowned,

Bathed and buried in the bright
Warm luxuriance of light, —
Fair the hills without a stain.

Fairer far the hills should stand
Crownèd with a city's halls,
With the glimmer of white walls,
With the climbing grace of towers ;
Fair with great fronts tall and grand,
Stately streets that meet the sky,
Lovely roof-lines, low and high, —
Fairer for the days and hours.

Woman's beauty fades and flies,
In the passing of the years,
With the falling of the tears,
With the lines of toil and stress ;
City's beauty never dies, —
Never while her people know
How to love and honor so
Her immortal loveliness.

TWO SKIES.

FROM ENGLAND.

THEY have a sky in Albion,
At least they tell me so ;
But she will wear a veil so thick,

And she does have the sulks so quick,
  And weeps so long and slow,
  That one can hardly know.

Yes, there 's a sky in Albion.
  She 's shown herself of late.
And where it was not white or gray,
It was quite bluish — in a way ;
  But near and full of weight,
  Like an overhanging plate !

Our sky in California !
  Such light the angels knew,
When the strong, tender smile of God
Kindled the spaces where they trod,
  And made all life come true !
  Deep, soundless, burning blue !

WINDS AND LEAVES.
FROM ENGLAND.

WET winds that flap the sodden leaves !
Wet leaves that drop and fall !
Unhappy, leafless trees the wind bereaves !
  Poor trees and small !

All of a color, solemn in your green ;
All of a color, sombre in your brown ;
All of a color, dripping gray between
  When leaves are down !

O for the bronze-green eucalyptus spires
Far-flashing up against the endless blue!
Shifting and glancing in the steady fires
    Of sun and moonlight too.

Dark orange groves! Pomegranate hedges bright,
And varnished fringes of the pepper trees!
And O that wind of sunshine! Wind of light!
    Wind of Pacific seas!

ON THE PAWTUXET.

BROAD and blue is the river, all bright in the sun;
The little waves sparkle, the little waves run;
The birds carol high, and the winds whisper low;
The boats beckon temptingly, row upon row:
Her hand is in mine as I help her step in.
Please Heaven, this day I shall lose or shall win —
    Broad and blue is the river.

Cool and gray is the river, the sun sinks apace,
And the rose-colored twilight glows soft in her face.
In the midst of the rose-color Venus doth shine,
And the blossoming wild grapes are sweeter than
    wine;
Tall trees rise above us, four bridges are past,
And my stroke 's running slow as the current runs
    fast —
    Cool and gray is the river.

Smooth and black is the river, no sound as we float
Save the soft-lapping water in under the boat.
The white mists are rising, the moon's rising too,
And Venus, triumphant, rides high in the blue.
I hold the shawl round her, her hand is in mine,
And we drift under grape-blossoms sweeter than
    wine —
        Smooth and black is the river.

A MOONRISE.

THE heavy mountains, lying huge and dim,
With uncouth outline breaking heaven's brim ;
And while I watched and waited, o'er them soon,
Cloudy, enormous, spectral, rose the moon.

THEIR GRASS!

A PROTEST FROM CALIFORNIA.

THEY say we have no grass !
To hear them talk
You 'd think that grass could walk
And was their bosom friend, — no day to pass
Between them and their grass.

"No grass !" they say who live
Where hot bricks give
The hot stones all their heat and back again, —
A baking hell for men.

"O, but," they haste to say, "we have our parks,
Where fat policemen check the children's larks;
And sign to sign repeats as in a glass,
    'Keep off the grass!'
We have our cities' parks and grass, you see!"
Well — so have we!

But 'tis the country that they sing of most. "Alas,"
They sing, "for our wide acres of soft grass!—
To please us living and to hide us dead—"
You'd think Walt Whitman's first was all they read!
You'd think they all went out upon the quiet
Nebuchadnezzar to outdo in diet!
You'd think they found no other green thing fair,
Even its seed an honor in their hair!
You'd think they had this bliss the whole year
    round, —
Evergreen grass! — and we, ploughed ground!

But come now, how does earth's pet plumage grow
Under your snow?
Is your beloved grass as softly nice
When packed in ice?
For six long months you live beneath a blight, —
No grass in sight.
You bear up bravely. And not only that,
But leave your grass and travel; and thereat
We marvel deeply, with slow western mind,
Wondering within us what these people find

Among our common oranges and palms
To tear them from the well-remembered charms
Of their dear vegetable.   But still they come,
Frost-bitten invalids ! to our bright home,
And chide our grasslessness !   Until we say,
" But if you hate it so, why come ?   Why stay ?
Just go away !
Go to — your grass ! "

THE PROPHETS.

TIME was we stoned the Prophets.   Age on age,
When men were strong to save, the world hath
     slain them.
People are wiser now ; they waste no rage —
     The Prophets entertain them !

SIMILAR CASES.

THERE was once a little animal,
    No bigger than a fox,
And on five toes he scampered
    Over Tertiary rocks.
They called him Eohippus,
    And they called him very small,
And they thought him of no value —
    When they thought of him at all;

95

For the lumpish old Dinoceras
And Coryphodon so slow
Were the heavy aristocracy
In days of long ago.

Said the little Eohippus,
"I am going to be a horse!
And on my middle finger-nails
To run my earthly course!
I 'm going to have a flowing tail!
I 'm going to have a mane!
I 'm going to stand fourteen hands high
On the psychozoic plain!"

The Coryphodon was horrified,
The Dinoceras was shocked;
And they chased young Eohippus,
But he skipped away and mocked.
Then they laughed enormous laughter,
And they groaned enormous groans,
And they bade young Eohippus
Go view his father's bones.
Said they, "You always were as small
And mean as now we see,
And that 's conclusive evidence
That you 're always going to be.
What! Be a great, tall, handsome beast,
With hoofs to gallop on?

Why !   You 'd have to change your nature ! "
  Said the Loxolophodon.
They considered him disposed of,
  And retired with gait serene;
That was the way they argued
  In " the early Eocene."

There was once an Anthropoidal Ape,
  Far smarter than the rest,
And everything that they could do
  He always did the best;
So they naturally disliked him,
  And they gave him shoulders cool,
And when they had to mention him
  They said he was a fool.

Cried this pretentious Ape one day,
  " I 'm going to be a Man !
And stand upright, and hunt, and fight,
  And conquer all I can !
I 'm going to cut down forest trees,
  To make my houses higher !
I 'm going to kill the Mastodon !
  I 'm going to make a fire ! "

Loud screamed the Anthropoidal Apes
  With laughter wild and gay;
They tried to catch that boastful one,
  But he always got away.

So they yelled at him in chorus,
  Which he minded not a whit;
And they pelted him with cocoanuts,
  Which did n't seem to hit.
And then they gave him reasons
  Which they thought of much avail,
To prove how his preposterous
  Attempt was sure to fail.
Said the sages, " In the first place,
  The thing cannot be done !
And, second, if it *could* be,
  It would not be any fun !
And, third, and most conclusive,
  And admitting no reply,
You would have to change your nature !
  We should like to see you try ! "
They chuckled then triumphantly,
  These lean and hairy shapes,
For these things passed as arguments
  With the Anthropoidal Apes.

There was once a Neolithic Man,
  An enterprising wight,
Who made his chopping implements
  Unusually bright.
Unusually clever he,
  Unusually brave,
And he drew delightful Mammoths

On the borders of his cave.
To his Neolithic neighbors,
  Who were startled and surprised,
Said he, " My friends, in course of time,
  We shall be civilized !
We are going to live in cities !
  We are going to fight in wars !
We are going to eat three times a day
  Without the natural cause !
We are going to turn life upside down
  About a thing called gold !
We are going to want the earth, and take
  As much as we can hold !
We are going to wear great piles of stuff
  Outside our proper skins !
We are going to have Diseases !
  And Accomplishments ! ! And Sins ! ! ! "

Then they all rose up in fury
  Against their boastful friend,
For prehistoric patience
  Cometh quickly to an end.
Said one, " This is chimerical !
  Utopian ! Absurd ! "
Said another, " What a stupid life !
  Too dull, upon my word ! "
Cried all, " Before such things can come,
  You idiotic child,

You must alter Human Nature ! ''
And they all sat back and smiled.
Thought they, " An answer to that last
It will be hard to find ! ''
It was a clinching argument
To the Neolithic Mind !

A CONSERVATIVE.

THE garden beds I wandered by
One bright and cheerful morn,
When I found a new-fledged butterfly
A-sitting on a thorn,
A black and crimson butterfly,
All doleful and forlorn.

I thought that life could have no sting
To infant butterflies,
So I gazed on this unhappy thing
With wonder and surprise,
While sadly with his waving wing
He wiped his weeping eyes.

Said I, " What can the matter be ?
Why weepest thou so sore ?
With garden fair and sunlight free
And flowers in goodly store — ''
But he only turned away from me
And burst into a roar.

100

Cried he, " My legs are thin and few
  Where once I had a swarm !
Soft fuzzy fur — a joy to view —
  Once kept my body warm,
Before these flapping wing-things grew,
  To hamper and deform ! "

At that outrageous bug I shot
  The fury of mine eye ;
Said I, in scorn all burning hot,
  In rage and anger high,
" You ignominious idiot !
  Those wings are made to fly ! "

" I do not want to fly," said he,
  " I only want to squirm ! "
And he drooped his wings dejectedly,
  But still his voice was firm :
" I do not want to be a fly !
  I want to be a worm ! "

O yesterday of unknown lack !
  To-day of unknown bliss !
I left my fool in red and black,
  The last I saw was this, —
The creature madly climbing back
  Into his chrysalis.

AN OBSTACLE.

I was climbing up a mountain-path
  With many things to do,
Important business of my own,
  And other people's too,
When I ran against a Prejudice
  That quite cut off the view.

My work was such as could not wait,
  My path quite clearly showed,
My strength and time were limited,
  I carried quite a load;
And there that hulking Prejudice
  Sat all across the road.

So I spoke to him politely,
  For he was huge and high,
And begged that he would move a bit
  And let me travel by.
He smiled, but as for moving! —
  He did n't even try.

'And then I reasoned quietly
  With that colossal mule :
My time was short — no other path —
  The mountain winds were cool.
I argued like a Solomon ;
  He sat there like a fool.

Then I flew into a passion,
  I danced and howled and swore.
I pelted and belabored him
  Till I was stiff and sore;
He got as mad as I did —
  But he sat there as before.

And then I begged him on my knees;
  I might be kneeling still
If so I hoped to move that mass
  Of obdurate ill-will —
As well invite the monument
  To vacate Bunker Hill !

So I sat before him helpless,
  In an ecstasy of woe —
The mountain mists were rising fast,
  The sun was sinking slow —
When a sudden inspiration came,
  As sudden winds do blow.

I took my hat, I took my stick,
  My load I settled fair,
I approached that awful incubus
  With an absent-minded air —
And I walked directly through him,
  As if he was n't there !

THE FOX WHO HAD LOST HIS TAIL.

THE fox who had lost his tail found out
    That now he could faster go ;
He had less to cover when hid for prey,
He had less to carry on hunting day,
He had less to guard when he stood at bay;
    He was really better so !

Now he was a fine altruistical fox
    With the good of his race at heart,
So he ran to his people with tailless speed,
To tell of the change they all must need,
And recommend as a righteous deed
    That they and their tails should part !

Plain was the gain as plain could be,
    But his words did not avail ;
For they all replied, " We perceive your case ;
You do not speak for the good of the race,
But only to cover your own disgrace,
    Because you have lost your tail ! "

Then another fox, of a liberal mind,
    With a tail of splendid size,
Became convinced that the tailless state
Was better for all of them, soon or late.
Said he, " I will let my own tail wait,
    And so I can open their eyes."

Plain was the gain as plain could be,
 But his words did not avail,
For they all made answer, " My plausible friend,
You talk wisely and well, but you talk to no end.
We know you 're dishonest and only pretend,
 For you have not lost your tail ! "

THE SWEET USES OF ADVERSITY.

In Norway fiords, in summer-time,
 The Norway birch is fair :
The white trunks shine, the green leaves twine,
The whole tree groweth tall and fine ;
 For all it wants is there, —
 Water and warmth and air, —
Full fed in all its nature needs, and showing
That nature in perfection by its growing.

But follow the persistent tree
 To the limit of endless snow
There you may see what a birch can be !
The product showeth plain and free
 How nobly plants can grow
 With nine months' winter slow.
'T is fitted to survive in that position,
Developed by the force of bad condition.

See now what life the tree doth keep, —
 Branchless, three-leaved, and tough ;

In June the leaf-buds peep, flowers in July dare creep
To bloom, the fruit in August, and then sleep.
    Strong is the tree and rough,
    It lives, and that's enough.
"Dog's-ear" the name the peasants call it by —
A Norway birch — and less than one inch high!

.   .   .   .

That silver monarch of the summer wood,
Tall, straight, and lovely, rich in all things good,
    Knew not in his perversity
    The sweeter uses of adversity!

CONNOISSEURS.

"No," said the Cultured Critic, gazing haughtily
Whereon some untrained brush had wandered
        naughtily,
    From canons free ;
"Work such as this lacks value and perspective,
Has no real feeling, — inner or reflective, —
    Does not appeal to me."

Then quoth the vulgar, knowing art but meagrely,
Their unbesought opinions airing eagerly,
    "Why, ain't that flat?"
Voicing their ignorance all unconcernedly,
Saying of what the Critic scored so learnedly,
    "I don't like that!"

The Critic now vouchsafed approval sparingly
Of what some genius had attempted daringly,
   "This fellow tries;
He handles his conception frankly, feelingly.
Such work as this, done strongly and appealingly,
   I recognize."

The vulgar, gazing widely and unknowingly,
Still volunteered their cheap impressions flowingly,
   "Oh, come and see!"
But all that they could say of art's reality
Was this poor voice of poorer personality,
   "Now, that suits me!"

TECHNIQUE.

COMETH to-day the very skilful man;
  Profoundly skilful in his chosen art;
All things that other men can do he can,
  And do them better. He is very smart.

Sayeth, "My work is here before you all;
  Come now with duly cultured mind to view it.
Here is great work, no part of it is small;
  Perceive how well I do it!

"I do it to perfection. Studious years
  Were spent to reach the pinnacle I've won;
Labor and thought are in my work, and tears.
  Behold how well 't is done!

" See with what power this great effect is shown;
See with what ease you get the main idea;
A master in my art, I stand alone;
Now you may praise, — I hear."

And I, " O master, I perceive your sway,
I note the years of study, toil, and strain
That brought the easy power you wield to-day,
The height you now attain.

" Freely your well-trained power I see you spend,
Such skill in all my life I never saw;
You have done nobly; but, my able friend,
What have you done it for?

" You have no doubt achieved your dearest end:
Your work is faultless to the cultured view.
You do it well, but, O my able friend,
What is it that you do?"

THE PASTELLETTE.

" THE pastelle is too strong," said he.
" Lo! I will make it fainter yet!"
And he wrought with tepid ecstasy
A pastellette.

A touch — a word — a tone half caught —
He softly felt and handled them;
Flavor of feeling — scent of thought —
Shimmer of gem —

That we may read, and feel as he
  What vague, pale pleasure we can get
From this mild, witless mystery, —
    The pastellette.

THE PIG AND THE PEARL.

SAID the Pig to the Pearl, "Oh, fie!
Tasteless, and hard, and dry —
    Get out of my sty!
Glittering, smooth, and clean,
You only seek to be seen!
I am dirty and big!
A virtuous, valuable pig.
For me all things are sweet
That I can possibly eat;
But you — how can you be good
Without being fit for food?
Not even food for me,
Who can eat all this you see,
No matter how foul and sour;
I revel from hour to hour
In refuse of great and small;
But you are no good at all,
And if I should gulp you, quick,
It would probably make me sick!"
Said the Pig to the Pearl, "Oh, fie!"
And she rooted her out of the sty.

A Philosopher chancing to pass
Saw the Pearl in the grass,
And laid hands on the same in a trice,
For the Pearl was a Pearl of Great Price.
Said he, "Madame Pig, if you knew
What a fool thing you do,
It would grieve even you!
Grant that pearls are not just to your taste,
Must you let them run waste?
You care only for hogwash, I know,
For your litter and you. Even so,
This tasteless hard thing which you scorn
Would buy acres of corn;
And apples, and pumpkins, and pease,
By the ton, if you please!
By the wealth which this pearl represents,
You could grow so immense —
You, and every last one of your young —.
That your fame would be sung
As the takers of every first prize,
For your flavor and size!
From even a Pig's point of view
The Pearl was worth millions to you.
Be a Pig — and a fool — (you must be them)
But try to know Pearls when you see them!"

POOR HUMAN NATURE.

I saw a meagre, melancholy cow,
Blessed with a starveling calf that sucked in vain;
Eftsoon he died. I asked the mother how —?
Quoth she, " Of every four there dieth twain ! "
    Poor bovine nature !

I saw a sickly horse of shambling gait,
Ugly and wicked, weak in leg and back,
Useless in all ways, in a wretched state.
  " We 're all poor creatures ! " said the sorry hack.
    Poor equine nature !

I saw a slow cat crawling on the ground,
Weak, clumsy, inefficient, full of fears,
The mice escaping from her aimless bound.
  Moaned she, " This truly is a vale of tears ! "
    Poor feline nature !

Then did I glory in my noble race,
Healthful and beautiful, alert and strong,
Rejoicing that we held a higher place
And need not add to theirs our mournful song, —
    Poor human nature !

OUR SAN FRANCISCO CLIMATE.

Said I to my friend from the East, —
A tenderfoot he, —

111

As I showed him the greatest and least
    Of our hills by the sea,
" How do you like our climate ? "
    And I smiled in my glee.

I showed him the blue of the hills,
    And the blue of the sky,
And the blue of the beautiful bay
    Where the ferry-boats ply ;
And " How do you like our climate ? "
    Securely asked I.

Then the wind blew over the sand,
    And the fog came down,
And the papers and dust were on hand
    All over the town.
" How do you like our climate ? "
    I cried with a frown.

On the corner we stood as we met
    Awaiting a car ;
Beneath us a vent-hole was set,
    As our street corners are —
And street corners in our San Francisco
    Are perceptible far.

He meant to have answered, of course,
    I could see that he tried ;
112

But he had not the strength of a horse,
    And before he replied
The climate rose up from that corner in force,
    And he died!

SAN FRANCISCO, 1895.

CRITICISM.

THE Critic eyed the sunset as the umber turned to
    gray,
    Slow fading in the somewhat foggy west;
To the color-cultured Critic 't was a very dull
    display,
" 'T is n't half so good a sunset as was offered yes-
    terday!
I wonder why," he murmured, as he sadly turned
    away,
    " The sunsets can't be always at their best! "

ANOTHER CREED.

ANOTHER creed! We 're all so pleased!
A gentle, tentative new creed. We 're eased
Of all those things we could not quite believe,
But would not give the lie to. Now perceive
How charmingly this suits us! Science even
Has naught against our modern views of Heaven;
And yet the most emotional of women
May find this creed a warm, deep sea to swim in.

8   113

Here 's something now so loose and large of fit
That all the churches may come under it,
And we may see upon the earth once more
A church united, — as we had before!
Before so much of precious blood was poured
That each in his own way might serve the Lord!
All wide divergence in sweet union sunk,
Like branches growing up into a trunk!

And in our intellectual delight
In this sweet formula that sets us right;
And controversial exercises gay
With those who still prefer a differing way;
And our glad effort to make known this wonder
And get all others to unite thereunder, —
We, joying in this newest, best of creeds,
Continue still to do our usual deeds!

THE LITTLE LION.

It was a little lion lay —
In wait he lay — he lay in wait.
Came those who said, " Pray come my way;
We joy to see a lion play,
 And laud his gait!"

The little lion mildly came —
In wait for prey — for prey in wait.

The people all adored his name,
And those who led him saw the same
    With hearts elate.

The little lion grew that day, —
In glee he went — he went in glee.
Said he, "I love to seek my prey,
But also love to see the way
    My prey seek me!"

A MISFIT.

O LORD, take me out of this!
        I do not fit!
My body does not suit my mind,
My brain is weak in the knees and blind,
My clothes are not what I want to find —
        Not one bit!

My house is not the house I like —
        Not one bit!
My church is built so loose and thin
That ten fall out where one falls in;
My creed is buttoned with a pin —
        It does not fit!

The school I went to was n't right —
        Not one bit!
The education given me

Was meant for the community,
And my poor head works differently —
It does not fit!

I try to move and find I can't —
Not one bit!
Things that were given me to stay
Are mostly lost and blown away,
And what I have to use to-day —
It does not fit!

What I was taught I cannot do —
Not one bit!
And what I do I was not taught
And what I find I have not sought;
I never say the thing I ought —
It does not fit!

I have not meant to be like this —
Not one bit!
But in the puzzle and the strife
I fail my friend and pain my wife;
Oh, how it hurts to have a life
That does not fit!

ON NEW YEAR'S DAY.

On New Year's Day he plans a cruise
To Heaven straight — no time to lose!

Vowing to live so virtuously
That each besetting sin shall flee —
Good resolutions wide he strews
    On New Year's Day.

A while he minds his p's and q's,
And all temptations doth refuse,
Recalling his resolves so free
    On New Year's Day.

But in the long year that ensues,
They fade away by threes and twos —
The place we do not wish to see
Is paved with all he meant to be,
When he next year his life reviews —
    On New Year's Day.

OUR EAST.

Our East, long looking backward over sea,
In loving study of what used to be,
Has grown to treat our West with the same scorn
England has had for us since we were born.

You 'd think to hear this Eastern judgment hard
The West was just New England's back yard!
That all the West was made for, last and least,
Was to raise pork and wheat to feed the East!

A place to travel in, for rest and health,
A place to struggle in and get the wealth,
The only normal end of which, of course,
Is to return to its historic source !

Our Western acres, curving to the sun,
The Western strength whereby our work is done,
All Western progress, they attribute fair
To Eastern Capital invested there !

New England never liked old England's scorn.
Do they think theirs more easy to be borne?
Or that the East, Britain's rebellious child,
Will find the grandson, West, more meek and
    mild ?

In union still our sovereignty has stood,
A union formed with prayer and sealed with blood.
We stand together. Patience, mighty West !
Don't mind this scolding from your last year's
    nest!

UNMENTIONABLE.

THERE is a thing of which I fain would speak,
        Yet shun the deed ;
Lest hot disgust flush the averted cheek
        Of those who read.

And yet it is as common in our sight
  As dust or grass;
Loathed by the lifted skirt, the tiptoe light,
  Of those who pass.

We say no word, but the big placard rests
  Frequent in view,
To sicken those who do not with requests
  Of those who do.

" Gentlemen will not," the mild placards say.
  They read with scorn.
" Gentlemen must not " — they defile the way
  Of those who warn.

On boat and car the careful lady lifts
  Her dress aside;
If careless — think, fair traveller, of the gifts
  Of those who ride!

On every hall and sidewalk, floor and stair,
  Where man 's at home,
This loathsomeness is added to the care
  Of those who come.

As some foul slug his trail of slime displays
  On leaf and stalk,
These street-beasts make a horror in the ways
  Of those who walk.

We cannot ask reform of those who do —
    They can't or won't.
We can express the scorn, intense and true,
    Of those who don't.

AN INVITATION FROM CALIFORNIA.

Are n't you tired of protection from the weather?
    Of defences, guards, and shields?
Are n't you tired of the worry as to whether
    This year the farm land yields?

Are n't you tired of the wetness and the dryness,
    The dampness, and the hotness, and the cold?
Of waiting on the weather man with shyness
    To see if the last plans hold?

Are n't you tired of the doctoring and nursing,
    Of the "sickly winters" and the pocket pills, —
Tired of sorrowing, and burying, and cursing
    At Providence and undertakers' bills?

Are n't you tired of all the threatening and doubt-
    ing,
    The "weather-breeder" with its lovely lie;
The dubiety of any sort of outing;
    The chip upon the shoulder of the sky?

THE WORLD.

Like a beaten horse who dodges your caresses,
Like a child abused who ducks before your frown,
Is the northerner in our warm air that blesses —
O come and live and take your elbow down!

Don't be afraid; you do not need defences;
This heavenly day breeds not a stormy end;
Lay down your arms! cut off your war expenses!
This weather is your friend!

A friendliness from earth, a joy from heaven,
A peace that wins your frightened soul at length;
A place where rest as well as work is given, —
Rest is the food of strength.

RESOLVE.

To keep my health!
To do my work!
To live!
To see to it I grow and gain and give!
Never to look behind me for an hour!
To wait in weakness, and to walk in power;
But always fronting onward to the light,
Always and always facing toward the right.
Robbed, starved, defeated, fallen, wide astray —
On, with what strength I have!
Back to the way!

121

WOMAN.

SHE WALKETH VEILED AND
SLEEPING.

[handwritten annotation: sheltered women — oblivious to potential.]

SHE walketh veiled and sleeping,
For she knoweth not her power;
She obeyeth but the pleading
Of her heart, and the high leading
Of her soul, unto this hour.
Slow advancing, halting, creeping,
Comes the Woman to the hour ! —
She walketh veiled and sleeping,
For she knoweth not her power.

TO MAN.

IN dark and early ages, through the primal forests
    faring,
Ere the soul came shining into prehistoric night,
Two-fold man was equal; they were comrades dear
    and daring,
Living wild and free together in unreasoning delight.

Ere the soul was born and consciousness came
    slowly,
Ere the soul was born, to man and woman too,
Ere he found the Tree of Knowledge, that awful
    tree and holy,
Ere he knew he felt, and knew he knew.

Then said he to Pain, "I am wise now, and I know
    you!
No more will I suffer while power and wisdom
    last!"
Then said he to Pleasure, "I am strong, and I will
    show you
That the will of man can seize you; aye, and hold
    you fast!"

Food he ate for pleasure, and wine he drank for
    gladness,
And woman? Ah, the woman! the crown of all
    delight! —
His now — he knew it! He was strong to madness
In that early dawning after prehistoric night.

His — his forever! That glory sweet and tender!
Ah, but he would love her! And she should love
    but him!
He would work and struggle for her, he would
    shelter and defend her;
She should never leave him, never, till their eyes
    in death were dim.

Close, close he bound her, that she should leave
    him never;
Weak still he kept her, lest she be strong to flee;
And the fainting flame of passion he kept alive
    forever
With all the arts and forces of earth and sky and sea.

And, ah, the long journey! The slow and awful
    ages
They have labored up together, blind and crippled,
    all astray!
Through what a mighty volume, with a million
    shameful pages,
From the freedom of the forest to the prisons of
    to-day!

Food he ate for pleasure, and it slew him with
    diseases!
Wine he drank for gladness, and it led the way to
    crime!
And woman? He will hold her — he will have
    her when he pleases —
And he never once hath seen her since the pre-
    historic time!

Gone the friend and comrade of the day when life
    was younger,
She who rests and comforts, she who helps and
    saves;
Still he seeks her vainly, with a never-dying hunger;
Alone beneath his tyrants, alone above his slaves!

Toiler, bent and weary with the load of thine own
    making!
Thou who art sad and lonely, though lonely all in
    vain!

Who hast sought to conquer Pleasure and have her
    for the taking,
And found that Pleasure only was another name
    for Pain, —

Nature hath reclaimed thee, forgiving dispossession!
God hath not forgotten, though man doth still for-
    get!
The woman-soul is rising, in despite of thy trans-
    gression;
Loose her now — and trust her! She will love thee
    yet!

Love thee? She will love thee as only freedom
    knoweth;
Love thee? She will love thee while Love itself
    doth live!
Fear not the heart of woman! No bitterness it
    showeth!
The ages of her sorrow have but taught her to
    forgive!

WOMEN OF TO-DAY.

You women of to-day who fear so much
The women of the future, showing how
The dangers of her course are such and such —
      What are you now?

Mothers and Wives and Housekeepers, forsooth !
Great names ! you cry, full scope to rule and please !
Room for wise age and energetic youth ! —
      But are you these ?

Housekeepers ?   Do you then, like those of yore,
Keep house with power and pride, with grace and
    ease ?
No, you keep servants only !   What is more,
      You don't keep these !

Wives, say you ?   Wives !   Blessed indeed are they
Who hold of love the everlasting keys,
Keeping their husbands' hearts !   Alas the day !
      You don't keep these !

And mothers ?   Pitying Heaven !   Mark the cry
From cradle death-beds !   Mothers on their knees !
Why, half the children born — as children die !
      You don't keep these !

And still the wailing babies come and go,
And homes are waste, and husbands' hearts fly far,
There is no hope until you dare to know
      The thing you are !

TO THE YOUNG WIFE.

ARE you content, you pretty three-years' wife ?
  Are you content and satisfied to live
  On what your loving husband loves to give,
    And give to him your life ?

9   129

IN THIS OUR WORLD.

Are you content with work, — to toil alone,
 To clean things dirty and to soil things clean;
 To be a kitchen-maid, be called a queen, —
   Queen of a cook-stove throne?

Are you content to reign in that small space —
 A wooden palace and a yard-fenced land —
 With other queens abundant on each hand,
  Each fastened in her place?

Are you content to rear your children so?
 Untaught yourself, untrained, perplexed, dis-
  tressed, *fear builds — anger*
 Are you so sure your way is always best?
  That you can always know?

Have you forgotten how you used to long
 In days of ardent girlhood, to be great,
 To help the groaning world, to serve the state,
  To be so wise — so strong?

And are you quite convinced this is the way,
 The only way a woman's duty lies —
 Knowing all women so have shut their eyes?
  Seeing the world to-day?

Have you no dream of life in fuller store?
 Of growing to be more than that you are?
 Doing the things you now do better far,
  Yet doing others — more?

130

[handwritten top left: Love Ew. Dickinson.]

[handwritten top right: Questioning Womanhood — Joyful tone belieing the message underneath.]

WOMAN.

Losing no love, but finding as you grew
    That as you entered upon nobler life
    You so became a richer, sweeter wife,
        A wiser mother too?

[handwritten right: Words rebellion — frustration, anger.]

What holds you? Ah, my dear, it is your throne,
    Your paltry queenship in that narrow place,
    Your antique labors, your restricted space,
        Your working all alone !

[handwritten: Majesty]

[handwritten: images of imprisonment]

Be not deceived ! 'T is not your wifely bond
    That holds you, nor the mother's royal power,
    But selfish, slavish service hour by hour —
        A life with no beyond !

[handwritten right: Caliban ?]

[handwritten: No future of Passivity.]

FALSE PLAY.

" Do you love me?" asked the mother of her child,
    And the baby answered, " No ! "
Great Love listened and sadly smiled ;
He knew the love in the heart of the child —
    That you could not wake it so.

" Do not love me?" the foolish mother cried,
    And the baby answered, " No ! "
He knew the worth of the trick she tried —
Great Love listened, and grieving, sighed
    That the mother scorned him so.

"Oh, poor mama ! " and she played her part
　　Till the baby's strength gave way :
He knew it was false in his inmost heart,
But he could not bear that her tears should start,
　　So he joined in the lying play.

" Then love mama ! " and the soft lips crept
　　To the kiss that his love should show, —
The mouth to speak while the spirit slept !
Great Love listened, and blushed, and wept
　　That they blasphemed him so.

MOTHERHOOD.

MOTHERHOOD : First mere laying of an egg,
With blind foreseeing of the wisest place,
And blind provision of the proper food
For unseen larva to grow fat upon
After the instinct-guided mother died, —
Posthumous motherhood, no love, no joy.

Motherhood : Brooding patient o'er the nest,
With gentle stirring of an unknown love ;
Defending eggs unhatched, feeding the young
For days of callow feebleness, and then
Driving the fledglings from the nest to fly.

Motherhood : When the kitten and the cub
Cried out alive, and first the mother knew

The fumbling of furry little paws,
The pressure of the hungry little mouths
Against the more than ready mother-breast, —
The love that comes of giving and of care.

Motherhood: Nursing with her heart-warm milk,
Fighting to death all danger to her young,
Hunting for food for little ones half-weaned,
Teaching them how to hunt and fight in turn, —
Then loving not till the new litter came.

Motherhood: When the little savage grew
Tall at his mother's side, and learned to feel
Some mother even in his father's heart,
Love coming to new babies while the first
Still needed mother's care, and therefore love, —
Love lasting longer because childhood did.

Motherhood: Semi-civilized, intense,
Fierce with brute passion, narrow with the range
Of slavish lives to meanest service bowed;
Devoted — to the sacrifice of life;
Jealous beyond belief, and ignorant
Even of what should keep the child alive.
Love spreading with the spread of human needs,
The child's new, changing, ever-growing wants,
Yet seeking like brute mothers of the past
To give all things to her own child herself.
Loving to the exclusion of all else;

To the child's service bending a whole life ;
Yet stunting the young creature day by day
With lack of Justice, Liberty, and Peace.

Motherhood: Civilized. There stands at last,
Facing the heavens with as calm a smile,
The highest fruit of the long work of God ;
The highest type of this, the highest race ;
She from whose groping instinct grew all love —
All love — in which is all the life of man.

Motherhood: Seeing with her clear, kind eyes,
Luminous, tender eyes, wherein the smile
Is like the smile of sunlight on the sea,
That the new children of the newer day
Need more than any single heart can give,
More than is known to any single mind,
More than is found in any single house,
And need it from the day they see the light.
Then, measuring her love by what they need,
Gives, from the heart of modern motherhood.
Gives first, as tree to bear God's highest fruit,
A clean, strong body, perfect and full grown,
Fair for the purpose of its womanhood,
Not for light fancy of a lower mind ;
Gives a clear mind, athletic, beautiful,
Dispassionate, unswerving from the truth ;
Gives a great heart that throbs with human love,
As she would wish her son to love the world.

Then, when the child comes, lovely as a star,
She, in the peace of primal motherhood,
Nurses her baby with unceasing joy,
With milk of human kindness, human health,
Bright human beauty, and immortal love.
And then ? Ah ! here is the New Motherhood —
The motherhood of the fair new-made world —
O glorious New Mother of New Men !
Her child, with other children from its birth,
In the unstinted freedom of warm air,
Under the wisest eyes, the tenderest thought,
Surrounded by all beauty and all peace,
Led, playing, through the gardens of the world,
With the crowned heads of science and great love
Mapping safe paths for those small, rosy feet, —
Taught human love by feeling human love,
Taught justice by the laws that rule his days,
Taught wisdom by the way in which he lives,
Taught to love all mankind and serve them fair
By seeing, from his birth, all children served
With the same righteous, all-embracing care.

O Mother ! Noble Mother, yet to come !
How shall thy child point to the bright career
Of her of whom he boasts to be the son —
Not for assiduous service spent on him,
But for the wisdom which has set him forth
A clear-brained, pure-souled, noble-hearted man,

With health and strength and beauty his by birth;
And, more, for the wide record of her life,
Great work, well done, that makes him praise her
    name
And long to make as great a one his own !
And how shall all the children of the world,
Feeling all mothers love them, loving all,
Rise up and call her blessed !
      This shall be.

SIX HOURS A DAY.

Six hours a day the woman spends on food !
Six mortal hours a day.   .   .   .   .
With fire and water toiling, heat and cold ;
Struggling with laws she does not understand
Of chemistry and physics, and the weight
Of poverty and ignorance besides,
Toiling for those she loves, the added strain
Of tense emotion on her humble skill,
The sensitiveness born of love and fear,
Making it harder to do even work.
Toiling without release, no hope ahead
Of taking up another business soon,
Of varying the task she finds too hard —
This, her career, so closely interknit
With holier demands as deep as life
That to refuse to cook is held the same

As to refuse her wife and motherhood.
Six mortal hours a day to handle food, —
Prepare it, serve it, clean it all away, —
With allied labors of the stove and tub,
The pan, the dishcloth, and the scrubbing-brush.
Developing forever in her brain
The power to do this work in which she lives;
While the slow finger of Heredity
Writes on the forehead of each living man,
Strive as he may, " His mother was a cook ! "

AN OLD PROVERB.

" As much pity to see a woman weep as to see a goose go barefoot."

No escape, little creature ! The earth hath no place
For the woman who seeketh to fly from her race.
Poor, ignorant, timid, too helpless to roam,
The woman must bear what befalls her, at home.
Bear bravely, bear dumbly — it is but the same
That all others endure who live under the name.
No escape, little creature !

No escape under heaven ! Can man treat you worse
After God has laid on you his infinite curse ?
The heaviest burden of sorrow you win
Cannot weigh with the load of original sin ;
No shame be too black for the cowering face
Of her who brought shame to the whole human race !
No escape under heaven !

Yet you feel, being human.   You shrink from the
    pain
That each child, born a woman, must suffer again.
From the strongest of bonds heart can feel, man
    can shape,
You cannot rebel, or appeal, or escape.
You must bear and endure.   If the heart cannot
    sleep,
And the pain groweth bitter, — too bitter, — then
    weep!
        For you feel, being human.

And she wept, being woman.   The numberless
    years
Have counted her burdens and counted her tears;
The maid wept forsaken, the mother forlorn
For the child that was dead, and the child that was
    born.
Wept for joy — as a miracle! — wept in her pain!
Wept aloud, wept in secret, wept ever in vain!
        Still she weeps, being woman.

REASSURANCE.

Can you imagine nothing better, brother,
Than that which you have always had before?
Have you been so content with " wife and mother,"
    You dare hope nothing more?

WOMAN.

Have you forever prized her, praised her, sung her,
The happy queen of a most happy reign?
Never dishonored her, despised her, flung her
    Derision and disdain?

Go ask the literature of all the ages!
Books that were written before women read!
Pagan and Christian, satirists and sages, —
    Read what the world has said!

There was no power on earth to bid you slacken
The generous hand that painted her disgrace!
There was no shame on earth too black to blacken
    That much praised woman-face!

Eve and Pandora! — always you begin it —
The ancients called her Sin and Shame and Death!
"There is no evil without woman in it,"
    The modern proverb saith!

She has been yours in uttermost possession, —
Your slave, your mother, your well-chosen bride,—
And you have owned, in million-fold confession,
    You were not satisfied.

Peace, then! Fear not the coming woman, brother!
Owning herself, she giveth all the more!
She shall be better woman, wife, and mother
    Than man hath known before!

MOTHER TO CHILD.

How best can I serve thee, my child! My child!
Flesh of my flesh and dear heart of my heart!
Once thou wast within me — I held thee — I fed
    thee —
By the force of my loving and longing I led thee —
      Now we are apart!

I may blind thee with kisses and crush with em-
    bracing,
Thy warm mouth in my neck and our arms inter-
    lacing;
But here in my body my soul lives alone,
And thou answerest me from a house of thine own,—
      That house which I builded!

Which we builded together, thy father and I;
In which thou must live, O my darling, and die!
Not one stone can I alter, one atom relay, —
Not to save or defend thee or help thee to stay —
      That gift is completed!

How best can I serve thee? O child, if they knew
How my heart aches with loving! How deep and
    how true,
How brave and enduring, how patient, how strong,
How longing for good and how fearful of wrong,
      Is the love of thy mother!

WOMAN.

Could I crown thee with riches !   Surround, over-
   flow thee
With fame and with power till the whole world
   should know thee ;
With wisdom and genius to hold the world still,
To bring laughter and tears, joy and pain, at thy will,
     Still — *thou* mightst not be happy !

Such have lived — and in sorrow.   The greater the
   mind,
The wider and deeper the grief it can find.
The richer, the gladder, the more thou canst feel
The keen stings that a lifetime is sure to reveal.
      O my child !   Must thou suffer ?

Is there no way my life can save thine from a pain ?
Is the love of a mother no possible gain ?
No labor of Hercules — search for the Grail —
No way for this wonderful love to avail ?
      God in Heaven — O teach me !

My prayer has been answered.   The pain thou must
   bear
Is the pain of the world's life which thy life must
   share.
Thou art one with the world — though I love thee
   the best ;
And to save thee from pain I must save all the rest —
     Well — with God's help I 'll do it !

Thou art one with the rest. I must love thee in them.
Thou wilt sin with the rest; and thy mother must
    stem
The world's sin. Thou wilt weep; and thy mother
    must dry
The tears of the world lest her darling should cry.
    I will do it — God helping !

And I stand not alone. I will gather a band
Of all loving mothers from land unto land.
Our children are part of the world ! do ye hear ?
They are one with the world — we must hold them
    all dear !
    Love all for the child's sake !

For the sake of my child I must hasten to save
All the children on earth from the jail and the grave.
For so, and so only, I lighten the share
Of the pain of the world that my darling must bear —
    Even so, and so only !

SERVICES.

Sнɛ was dead. Forth went the word,
And every creature heard.
To the last hamlet in the farthest lands,
To people countless as the sands
Of primal seas.

142

And with the word so sent
Her life's full record went, —
Of what fair line, how gifted, how endowed,
How educated ; and then, told aloud,
The splendid tale of what her life had done;
And all the people heard and felt as one ;
Exulting all together in their dead,
And the grand story of the life she led.

But in the city where her body lay
Great services were held on that fair day :
People by thousands ; music to the sky ;
Flowers of a garnered season ; winding by,
Processions, glorious in rich array,
All massing in the temple where she lay.

Then, when the music rested, rose and stood
Those who could speak of her and count the good,
The measureless great good her life had spread,
That all might hear the praises of their dead.
And those who loved her sent from the world's end
Their tribute to the memory of their friend;
While teachers to their children whispered low,
" See that you have as many when you go ! "

Then was recited how her life had part
In building up this science and that art,
Inventing here, administering there,
Helping to organize, create, prepare,

With fullest figures to expatiate
On her unmeasured value to the state.
And the child, listening, grew in noble pride,
And planned for greater praises when he died.

Then the Poet spoke of those long ripening years;
And tenderer music brought the grateful tears ;
And then, lest grief upon their heartstrings hang,
Her children stood around the bier and sang :

> In the name of the mother that bore us —
> Bore us strong — bore us free —
> We will strive in the labors before us,
> Even as she ! Even as she !

> In the name of her wisdom and beauty,
> Of her life full of light,
> We will live in our national duty,
> We will help on the right :

> We will love as her heart loved before us,
> Warm and wide — strong and high !
> In the name of the mother that bore us,
> We will live ! We will die !

IN MOTHER-TIME.

WHEN woman looks at woman with the glory in
her eyes,
When eternity lies open like a scroll,

WOMAN.

When immortal life is being felt, — the life that
    never dies, —
  And the triumph of it ringeth
  And the sweetness of it singeth
      In the soul,

Then we come to California, the Garden of the
    Lord,
Through all its leagues of endless blossoming;
And we sing, we sing together, to the whole world's
    deep accord —
  And we feel each other praying
  Over what the flowers are saying
      As we sing.

We were waiting, we were growing, glad of heart
    and strong of soul,
Like the peace and power of all these virgin lands;
Through the years of holy maidenhood with mother-
    hood for goal —
  And soon we shall be holding
  Fruit of all life's glad unfolding
      In our hands.

White-robed mothers, flower-crowned mothers, in
    the splendor of their youth,
In the grandeur of maturity and power;
Feeling life has passed the telling in its joyousness
    and truth,

10   145

Feeling life will soon be giving
Them the golden key of living
　　In one hour.

We come to California for the sunshine and the
　　flowers;
Our motherhood has brought us here as one;
For the fruit of all the ages should share the shining
　　hours,
　　With the blossoms ever-springing
　　And the golden globes low swinging,
　　　　In the sun.

SHE WHO IS TO COME.

A WOMAN — in so far as she beholdeth
　　Her one Beloved's face;
A mother — with a great heart that enfoldeth
　　The children of the Race;
A body, free and strong, with that high beauty
　　That comes of perfect use, is built thereof;
A mind where Reason ruleth over Duty,
　　And Justice reigns with Love;
A self-poised, royal soul, brave, wise, and tender,
　　No longer blind and dumb;
A Human Being, of an unknown splendor,
　　Is she who is to come!

GIRLS OF TO-DAY.

GIRLS of to-day ! Give ear !
Never since time began
Has come to the race of man
A year, a day, an hour,
So full of promise and power
   As the time that now is here !

Never in all the lands
Was there a power so great,
To move the wheels of state,
To lift up body and mind,
To waken the deaf and blind,
   As the power that is in your hands !

Here at the gates of gold
You stand in the pride of youth,
Strong in courage and truth,
Stirred by a force kept back
Through centuries long and black,
   Armed with a power threefold !

First : You are makers of men !
Then Be the things you preach !
Let your own greatness teach !
When mothers like this you see
Men will be strong and free —
   Then, and not till then !

147

Second : Since Adam fell,
Have you not heard it said
That men by women are led ?
True is the saying — true !
See to it what you do !
　See that you lead them well !

Third : You have work of your own !
Maid and mother and wife,
Look in the face of life !
There are duties you owe the race !
Outside your dwelling-place
　There is work for you alone !

Maid and mother and wife,
See your own work be done !
Be worthy a noble son !
Help man in the upward way !
Truly, a girl to-day
　Is the strongest thing in life !

" WE, AS WOMEN."

THERE 's a cry in the air about us —
　We hear it before, behind —
Of the way in which " We, as women,"
　Are going to lift mankind !

WOMAN.

With our white frocks starched and ruffled,
  And our soft hair brushed and curled —
Hats off! for " we, as women,"
  Are coming to help the world!

Fair sisters, listen one moment —
  And perhaps you 'll pause for ten :
The business of women as women
  Is only with men as men!

What we do, " we, as women,"
  We have done all through our life ;
The work that is ours as women
  Is the work of mother and wife!

But to elevate public opinion,
  And to lift up erring man,
Is the work of the Human Being ;
  Let us do it — if we can.

But wait, warm-hearted sisters —
  Not quite so fast, so far.
Tell me how we are going to lift a thing
  Any higher than we are!

We are going to " purify politics "
  And to " elevate the press."
We enter the foul paths of the world
  To sweeten and cleanse and bless.

To hear the high things we are going to do,
  And the horrors of man we tell,
One would think " we, as women," were angels,
  And our brothers were fiends of hell.

We, that were born of one mother,
  And reared in the selfsame place, —
In the school and the church together, —
  We, of one blood, one race !

Now then, all forward together !
  But remember, every one,
That it is not by feminine innocence
  The work of the world is done.

The world needs strength and courage,
  And wisdom to help and feed—
When " we, as women," bring these to man,
  We shall lift the world indeed !

IF MOTHER KNEW.

If mother knew the way I felt, —
  And I 'm sure a mother should, —
She would n't make it quite so hard
  For a person to be good !

I want to do the way she says ;
  I try to all day long ;
And then she just skips all the right,
  And pounces on the wrong !

WOMAN.

A dozen times I do a thing,
 And one time I forget;
And then she looks at me and asks
 If I can't remember yet?

She'll tell me to do something,
 And I'll really start to go;
But she'll keep right on telling it
 As if I did n't know.

Till it seems as if I could n't —
 It makes me kind of wild;
And then she says she never saw
 Such a disobliging child.

I go to bed all sorry,
 And say my prayers, and cry,
And mean next day to be so good
 I just can't wait to try.

And I get up next morning,
 And mean to do just right;
But mother's sure to scold me
 About something, before night.

I wonder if she really thinks
 A child could go so far,
As to be perfect all the time
 As the grown up people are!

If she only knew I tried to, —
And I 'm sure a mother should, —
She would n't make it quite so hard
For a person to be good!

THE ANTI-SUFFRAGISTS.

FASHIONABLE women in luxurious homes,
With men to feed them, clothe them, pay their bills,
Bow, doff the hat, and fetch the handkerchief;
Hostess or guest, and always so supplied
With graceful deference and courtesy;
Surrounded by their servants, horses, dogs, —
These tell us they have all the rights they want.

Successful women who have won their way
Alone, with strength of their unaided arm,
Or helped by friends, or softly climbing up
By the sweet aid of " woman's influence; "
Successful any way, and caring naught
For any other woman's unsuccess, —
These tell us they have all the rights they want.

Religious women of the feebler sort, —
Not the religion of a righteous world,
A free, enlightened, upward-reaching world,
But the religion that considers life
As something to back out of! — whose ideal

Is to renounce, submit, and sacrifice,
Counting on being patted on the head
And given a high chair when they get to heaven, —
These tell us they have all the rights they want.

Ignorant women — college-bred sometimes,
But ignorant of life's realities
And principles of righteous government,
And how the privileges they enjoy
Were won with blood and tears by those before —
Those they condemn, whose ways they now oppose;
Saying, " Why not let well enough alone?
Our world is very pleasant as it is," —
These tell us they have all the rights they want.

And selfish women, — pigs in petticoats, —
Rich, poor, wise, unwise, top or bottom round,
But all sublimely innocent of thought,
And guiltless of ambition, save the one
Deep, voiceless aspiration — to be fed !
These have no use for rights or duties more.
Duties to-day are more than they can meet,
And law insures their right to clothes and food, —
These tell us they have all the rights they want.

And, more 's the pity, some good women, too;
Good conscientious women, with ideas ;
Who think — or think they think — that woman's
    cause

Is best advanced by letting it alone;
That she somehow is not a human thing,
And not to be helped on by human means,
Just added to humanity — an " L " —
A wing, a branch, an extra, not mankind, —
These tell us they have all the rights they want.

And out of these has come a monstrous thing,
A strange, down-sucking whirlpool of disgrace,
Women uniting against womanhood,
And using that great name to hide their sin !
Vain are their words as that old king's command
Who set his will against the rising tide.
But who shall measure the historic shame
Of these poor traitors — traitors are they all —
To great Democracy and Womanhood !

WOMEN DO NOT WANT IT.

WHEN the woman suffrage argument first stood
    upon its legs,
They answered it with cabbages, they answered it
    with eggs,
They answered it with ridicule, they answered it
    with scorn,
They thought it a monstrosity that should not have
    been born.

When the woman suffrage argument grew vigorous
  and wise,
And was not to be silenced by these apposite
  replies,
They turned their opposition into reasoning severe
Upon the limitations of our God-appointed sphere.

We were told of disabilities, — a long array of these,
Till one would think that womanhood was merely
  a disease ;
And " the maternal sacrifice " was added to the plan
Of the various sacrifices we have always made —
  to man.

Religionists and scientists, in amity and bliss,
However else they disagreed, could all agree on this,
And the gist of all their discourse, when you got
  down to it,
Was — we could not have the ballot because we
  were not fit !

They would not hear to reason, they would not
  fairly yield,
They would not own their arguments were beaten
  in the field ;
But time passed on, and someway, we need not ask
  them how,
Whatever ails those arguments — we do not hear
  them now !

You may talk of woman suffrage now with an
    educated man,
And he agrees with all you say, as sweetly as he
    can ;
'T would be better for us all, of course, if woman-
    hood was free ;
But "the women do not want it" — and so it must
    not be !

'T is such a tender thoughtfulness ! So exquisite
    a care !
Not to pile on our fair shoulders what we do not
    wish to bear !
But, oh, most generous brother ! Let us look a little
    more —
Have we women always wanted what you gave to
    us before ?

Did we ask for veils and harems in the Oriental
    races ?
Did we beseech to be "unclean," shut out of sacred
    places ?
Did we beg for scolding bridles and ducking stools
    to come ?
And clamor for the beating stick no thicker than
    your thumb ?

Did we seek to be forbidden from all the trades
    that pay ?
Did we claim the lower wages for a man's full work
    to-day ?
Have we petitioned for the laws wherein our shame
    is shown :
That not a woman's child — nor her own body —
    is her own ?

What women want has never been a strongly act-
    ing cause
When woman has been wronged by man in churches,
    customs, laws ;
Why should he find this preference so largely in
    his way
When he himself admits the right of what we ask
    to-day ?

WEDDED BLISS.

"O come and be my mate!" said the Eagle to the
        Hen ;
    "I love to soar, but then
    I want my mate to rest
    Forever in the nest ! "
    Said the Hen, " I cannot fly,
    I have no wish to try,
But I joy to see my mate careering through the sky ! "
They wed, and cried, " Ah, this is Love, my own ! "
And the Hen sat, the Eagle soared, alone.

"O come and be my mate!" said the Lion to the
    Sheep;
  "My love for you is deep!
  I slay, a Lion should,
  But you are mild and good!"
  Said the Sheep, "I do no ill —
  Could not, had I the will —
But I joy to see my mate pursue, devour, and kill."
They wed, and cried, "Ah, this is Love, my own!"
And the Sheep browsed, the Lion prowled, alone.

"O come and be my mate!" said the Salmon to the
    Clam;
  "You are not wise, but I am.
  I know sea and stream as well;
  You know nothing but your shell."
  Said the Clam, "I'm slow of motion,
  But my love is all devotion,
And I joy to have my mate traverse lake and stream
    and ocean!"
They wed, and cried, "Ah, this is Love, my own!"
And the Clam sucked, the Salmon swam, alone.

THE HOLY STOVE.

O THE soap-vat is a common thing!
  The pickle-tub is low!
  The loom and wheel have lost their grace

WOMAN.

In falling from the dwelling-place
    To mills where all may go !
The bread-tray needeth not your love;
    The wash-tub wide doth roam ;
Even the oven free may rove;
But bow ye down to the Holy Stove,
    The Altar of the Home !

Before it bend the worshippers,
    And wreaths of parsley twine;
Above it still the incense curls,
And a passing train of hired girls
    Do service at the shrine.
We toil to keep the altar crowned
    With dishes new and nice,
And Art and Love, and Time and Truth,
We offer up, with Health and Youth,
    In daily sacrifice.

Speak not to us of a fairer faith,
    Of a lifetime free from pain.
Our fathers always worshipped here,
Our mothers served this altar drear,
    And still we serve amain.
Our earliest dreams around it cling,
    Bright hopes that childhood sees,
And memory leaves a vista wide
Where Mother's Doughnuts rank beside
    The thought of Mother's Knees.

The wood-box hath no sanctity;
   No glamour gilds the coal;
But the Cook-Stove is a sacred thing
To which a reverent faith we bring
   And serve with heart and soul.
The Home 's a temple all divine,
   By the Poker and the Hod !
The Holy Stove is the altar fine,
The wife the priestess at the shrine —
   Now who can be the god?

THE MOTHER'S CHARGE.

SHE raised her head. With hot and glittering eye,
"I know," she said, "that I am going to die.
Come here, my daughter, while my mind is clear.
Let me make plain to you your duty here;
My duty once — I never failed to try —
But for some reason I am going to die."
She raised her head, and, while her eyes rolled wild,
Poured these instructions on the gasping child:

" Begin at once — don't iron sitting down —
Wash your potatoes when the fat is brown —
Monday, unless it rains — it always pays
To get fall sewing done on the right days —
A carpet-sweeper and a little broom —
Save dishes — wash the summer dining-room

WOMAN.

With soda — keep the children out of doors —
The starch is out — beeswax on all the floors —
If girls are treated like your friends they stay —
They stay, and treat you like their friends — the way
To make home happy is to keep a jar —
And save the prettiest pieces for the star
In the middle — blue's too dark — all silk is best —
And don't forget the corners — when they're dressed
Put them on ice — and always wash the chest
Three times a day, the windows every week —
We need more flour — the bedroom ceilings leak —
It's better than onion — keep the boys at home —
Gardening is good — a load, three loads of loam —
They bloom in spring — and smile, smile always,
    dear —
Be brave, keep on — I hope I've made it clear."

She died, as all her mothers died before.
Her daughter died in turn, and made one more.

A BROOD MARE.

It is a significant fact that the phenomenal improvement in horses
during recent years is accompanied by the growing conviction that
good points and a good record are as desirable in the dam as in the
sire, if not more so.

    I HAD a quarrel yesterday,
        A violent dispute,
    With a man who tried to sell to me
        A strange amorphous brute;

A creature disproportionate,
A beast to make you stare,
An undeveloped, overgrown,
Outrageous-looking mare.

Her fore legs they were weak and thin,
Her hind legs weak and fat;
She was heavy in the quarters,
With a narrow chest and flat;

And she had managed to combine —
I 'm sure I don't know how —
The barrel of a greyhound
With the belly of a cow.

She seemed exceeding feeble,
And he owned with manner bland
That she walked a little, easily,
But was n't fit to stand.

I tried to mount the animal
To test her on the track;
But he cried in real anxiety,
" Get off!   You 'll strain her back!"

And then I sought to harness her,
But he explained at length
That any draught or carriage work
Was quite beyond her strength.

WOMAN.

"No use to carry or to pull!
No use upon the course!"
Said I, "How can you have the face
To call that thing a horse?"

Said he, indignantly, "I don't!
I 'm dealing on the square;
I never said it was a horse,
I told you 't was a mare!

"A mare was never meant to race,
To carry, or to pull;
She is meant for breeding only, so
Her place in life is full."

Said I, "Do you pretend to breed
From such a beast as that?
A mass of shapeless skin and bone,
Or shapeless skin and fat?"

Said he, "Her sire was thoroughbred,
As fine as walked the earth,
And all her colts receive from him
The marks of noble birth;

"And then I mate her carefully
With horses fine and fit;
Mares do not need to have themselves
The points which they transmit!"

Said I, " Do you pretend to say
  You can raise colts as fair
From that fat cripple as you can
  From an able-bodied mare ? "

Quoth he, " I solemnly assert,
  Just as I said before,
A mare that 's good for breeding
  Can be good for nothing more ! "

Cried I, " One thing is certain proof ;
  One thing I want to see ;
Trot out the noble colts you raise
  From your anomaly."

He looked a little dashed at this,
  And the poor mare hung her head.
" Fact is," said he, " she 's had but one,
  And that one — well, it 's dead ! "

FEMININE VANITY.

Feminine Vanity ! O ye Gods ! Hear to this man !
  As if silk and velvet and feathers and fur
  And jewels and gold had been just for her,
    Since the world began !

Where is his memory ? Let him look back — all
    of the way !
  Let him study the history of his race
  From the first he-savage that painted his face
    To the dude of to-day !

WOMAN.

Vanity! Oh! Are the twists and curls,
 The intricate patterns in red, black, and blue,
 The wearisome tortures of rich tattoo,
  Just made for girls?

Is it only the squaw who files the teeth,
 And dangles the lip, and bores the ear,
 And wears bracelet and necklet and anklet as
  queer
  As the bones beneath?

Look at the soldier, the noble, the king!
 Egypt or Greece or Rome discloses
 The purples and perfumes and gems and roses
  On a masculine thing!

Look at the men of our own dark ages!
 Heroes too, in their cloth of gold,
 With jewels as thick as the cloth could hold,
  On the knights and pages!

We wear false hair? Our man looks big!
 But it 's not so long, let me beg to state,
 Since every gentleman shaved his pate
  And wore a wig.

French heels? Sharp toes? See our feet defaced?
 But there was a day when the soldier free
 Tied the toe of his shoe to the manly knee —
  Yes, and even his waist!

We pad and stuff? Our man looks bolder.
Don't speak of the time when a bran-filled bunch
Made an English gentleman look like Punch —
   But feel of his shoulder!

Feminine Vanity! O ye Gods! Hear to these men!
Vanity 's wide as the world is wide!
Look at the peacock in his pride —
   Is it a hen?

THE MODEST MAID.

I AM a modest San Francisco maid,
   Fresh, fair, and young,
Such as the painters gladly have displayed,
   The poets sung.

Modest? — Oh, modest as a bud unblown,
   A thought unspoken;
Hidden and cherished, unbeheld, unknown,
   In peace unbroken.

Far from the holy shades of this my home,
   The coarse world raves,
And the New Woman cries to heaven's dome
   For what she craves.

Loud, vulgar, public, screaming from the stage,
   Her skirt divided,
Riding cross-saddled on the dying age,
   Justly derided.

WOMAN.

I blush for her, I blush for our sweet sex
　　By her disgraced.
My sphere is home.　My soul I do not vex
　　With zeal misplaced.

Come then to me with happy heart, O man !
　　I wait your visit.
To guide your footsteps I do all I can,
　　Am most explicit.

As veined flower-petals teach the passing bee
　　The way to honey,
So printer's ink displayed instructeth thee
　　Where lies my money.

Go see !　In type and cut across the page,
　　Before the nation,
There you may read about my eyes, my age,
　　My education,

My fluffy golden hair, my tiny feet,
　　My pet ambition,
My well-developed figure, and my sweet,
　　Retiring disposition.

All, all is there, and now I coyly wait.
　　Pray don't delay.
My address does the Blue Book plainly state,
　　And mamma's "day."

SAN FRANCISCO, 1895.

UNSEXED.

It was a wild rebellious drone
  That loudly did complain;
He wished he was a worker bee
  With all his might and main.

"I want to work," the drone declared.
  Quoth they, "The thing you mean
Is that you scorn to be a drone
  And long to be a queen.

"You long to lay unnumbered eggs,
  And rule the waiting throng;
You long to lead our summer flight,
  And this is rankly wrong."

Cried he, "My life is pitiful!
  I only eat and wed,
And in my marriage is the end —
  Thereafter I am dead.

"I would I were the busy bee
  That flits from flower to flower;
I long to share in work and care
  And feel the worker's power."

Quoth they, "The life you dare to spurn
  Is set before you here
As your one great, prescribed, ordained,
  Divinely ordered sphere!

" Without your services as drone,
  We should not be alive ;
Your modest task, when well fulfilled,
  Preserves the busy hive.

" Why underrate your blessed power ?
  Why leave your rightful throne
To choose a field of life that 's made
  For working bees alone ? "

Cried he, " But it is not enough,
  My momentary task !
Let me do that and more beside :
  To work is all I ask ! "

Then fiercely rose the workers all,
  For sorely were they vexed ;
" O wretch ! " they cried, " should this betide,
  You would become *unsexed* ! "

And yet he had not sighed for eggs,
  Nor yet for royal mien ;
He longed to be a worker bee,
  But not to be a queen.

FEMALES.

THE female fox she is a fox;
  The female whale a whale ;
The female eagle holds her place
As representative of race
  As truly as the male.

The mother hen doth scratch for her chicks,
  And scratch for herself beside;
The mother cow doth nurse her calf,
Yet fares as well as her other half
  In the pasture free and wide.

The female bird doth soar in air;
  The female fish doth swim;
The fleet-foot mare upon the course
Doth hold her own with the flying horse —
  Yea, and she beateth him!

One female in the world we find
  Telling a different tale.
It is the female of our race,
Who holds a parasitic place
  Dependent on the male.

Not so, saith she, ye slander me!
  No parasite am I!
I earn my living as a wife;
My children take my very life.
Why should I share in human strife.
  To plant and build and buy?

The human race holds highest place
  In all the world so wide,
Yet these inferior females wive,
And raise their little ones alive,
  And feed themselves beside.

The race is higher than the sex,
    Though sex be fair and good;
A Human Creature is your state,
And to be human is more great
    Than even womanhood!

The female fox she is a fox;
    The female whale a whale;
The female eagle holds her place
As representative of race
    As truly as the male.

A MOTHER'S SOLILOQUY.

You soft, pink, moving thing!
Young limbs that crave
Motion as free as zephyr-lifted wave;
Uneasy with the push of unlearned powers!
Exploring slowly through half-conscious hours;
With what rich new surprise and joy you feel
Your own will move yourself from head to heel!
So, let me swaddle you in bandage tight,
Dress you in wide, confining folds of white,
Cover you warmly, hold you close, and so
A mother's instinct-guided love I'll show!

Mysterious little frame!
Each organ new
And learning swiftly what it has to do!

Thy life's bright stream — as yet so newly thine —
Refreshed by heaven's sunlit air divine ;
With what delight you breathe in rosy ease
The strengthening, restful, blossom-scented breeze !
So, let me wrap you in a blanket shawl,
And veil your face in woollen, when at all
You meet the air.   Here in my arms is best
The curtained bedroom where your elders rest ;
So shall I guard you from a draught, and so
A mother's instinct-guided love I 'll show.

Young earnest mind at work !
Each sense attends
To teach you life's approaching foes and friends ;
Eye, ear, nose, tongue, and ever ready hand,
Eager to help you learn and understand.
What floods of happiness the day insures,
While each new knowledge is becoming yours !
So; let me firmly take away from you
The things you so persistently would view ;
And when you stretch the hand that tells so much,
Rap your soft knuckles and exclaim, " Don't touch ! "
I 'll tell you what you ought to learn, and so,
A mother's instinct-guided love I 'll show.

An ordinary child at best,
So neighbors tell ;
Not very large and strong, not very well ;

WOMAN.

A victim to the measles and the croup,
Fevers that flush and chill, and coughs that whoop;
To unknown naughtiness and well-known pain;
No racial progress here — no special gain!
But I, your mother, see with other eyes;
I hold you second to none under skies,
This estimate, unbased on any fact,
Shall teach you how to feel and how to act,
Shall make you wise, and true, and strong, and so,
A mother's instinct-guided love I'll show.

THEY WANDERED FORTH.

THEY wandered forth in springtime woods,
    Three women, thickly hung
With yards and yards of woollen goods —
    To play that they were young!

The river raced with the racing air;
    The woods were wild with song;
The glad birds darted everywhere —
    And so they walked along!

Stiff-bodied, fat, oppressed with cloth,
    Dull-colored, sad to see,
Slow-moving over the bright grass,
Their shapeless shadows fall and pass,
And dreaming not — alas! alas!
    Of what dear life might be!

BABY LOVE.

BABY LOVE came prancing by,
Cap on head and sword on thigh,
Horse to ride and drum to beat, —
All the world beneath his feet.

Mother Life was sitting there,
Hard at work and full of care,
Set of mouth and sad of eye.
Baby Love came prancing by.

Baby Love was very proud,
Very lively, very loud;
Mother Life arose in wrath,
Set an arm across his path.

Baby Love wept loud and long,
But his mother's arm was strong.
Mother had to work, she said.
Baby Love was put to bed.

THE MARCH.

THE WOLF AT THE DOOR.

THERE 's a haunting horror near us
    That nothing drives away :
Fierce lamping eyes at nightfall,
    A crouching shade by day ;
There 's a whining at the threshold,
    There 's a scratching at the floor.
To work ! To work ! In Heaven's name !
    The wolf is at the door !

The day was long, the night was short,
    The bed was hard and cold ;
Still weary are the little ones,
    Still weary are the old.
We are weary in our cradles
    From our mother's toil untold ;
We are born to hoarded weariness
    As some to hoarded gold.

We will not rise ! We will not work !
    Nothing the day can give
Is half so sweet as an hour of sleep ;
    Better to sleep than live !
What power can stir these heavy limbs ?
    What hope these dull hearts swell ?
What fear more cold, what pain more sharp,
    Than the life we know so well ?

To die like a man by lead or steel
    Is nothing that we should fear;
No human death would be worse to feel
    Than the life that holds us here.
But this is a fear no heart can face —
    A fate no man can dare —
To be run to earth and die by the teeth
    Of the gnawing monster there!

The slow, relentless, padding step
    That never goes astray —
The rustle in the underbrush —
    The shadow in the way —
The straining flight — the long pursuit —
    The steady gain behind —
Death-wearied man and tireless brute,
    And the struggle wild and blind!

There's a hot breath at the keyhole
    And a tearing as of teeth!
Well do I know the bloodshot eyes
    And the dripping jaws beneath!
There's a whining at the threshold —
    There's a scratching at the floor —
To work! To work! In Heaven's name!
    The wolf is at the door!

THE LOST GAME.

CAME the big children to the little ones,
  And unto them full pleasantly did say,
" Lo ! we have spread for you a merry game,
And ye shall all be winners at the same.
    Come now and play ! "

> *Great is the game they enter in, —*
> *Rouge et Noir on a giant scale, —*
> *Red with blood and black with sin,*
> *Where many must lose and few may win,*
> *And the players never fail !*

Said the strong children to the weaker ones,
  " See, ye are many, and we are but few !
The mass of all the counters ye divide,
But few remain to share upon our side.
    Play — as we do ! "

> *Strange is the game they enter in, —*
> *Rouge et Noir on a field of pain !*
> *And the silver white and the yellow gold*
> *Pile and pile in the victor's hold,*
> *While the many play in vain !*

Said the weak children to the stronger ones,
  " See now, howe'er it fall, we lose our share !
And play we well or ill we always lose;
While ye gain always more than ye can use.
    Bethink ye — is it fair ? "

Strange is the game they enter in, —
Rouge et Noir, and the bank is strong!
Play they well or play they wide
The gold is still on the banker's side,
And the game endureth long.

Said the strong children, each aside to each,
  " The game is slow — our gains are all too small ! "
Play we together now, 'gainst them apart ;
So shall these dull ones lose it from the start,
    And we shall gain it all ! "

Strange is the game that now they win, —
Rouge et Noir with a new design !
What can the many players do
Whose wits are weak and counters few
When the Power and the Gold combine?

Said the weak children to the stronger ones,
  " We care not for the game !
For play as we may our chance is small,
And play as ye may ye have it all.
    The end 's the same ! "

Strange is the game the world doth play, —
Rouge et Noir, with the counters gold,
Red with blood and black with sin ;
Few and fewer are they that win
As the ages pass untold.

THE MARCH.

Said the strong children to the weaker ones,
  " Ye lose in laziness ! ye lose in sleep !
Play faster now and make the counters spin !
Play well, as we, and ye in time shall win !
      Play fast ! Play deep ! "

        Strange is the game of Rouge et Noir, —
          Never a point have the little ones won.
        The winners are strong and flushed with gain,
        The losers are weak with want and pain,
          And still the game goes on.

But those rich players grew so very few,
  So many grew the poor ones, that one day
They rose up from that table, side by side,
Calm, countless, terrible — they rose and cried
In one great voice that shook the heavens wide,
      " WE WILL NOT PLAY ! "

        Where is the game of Rouge et Noir ?
        Where is the wealth of yesterday ?
        What availeth the power ye tell,
        And the skill in the game ye play so well ?
        If the players will not play ?

THE LOOKER-ON.

THE world was full of the battle,
  The whole world far and wide ;
Men and women and children
  Were fighting on either side.

181

I was sent from the hottest combat
    With a message of life and death,
Black with smoke and red with blood,
    Weary and out of breath,

Forced to linger a moment,
    And bind a stubborn wound,
Cursing the hurt that kept me back
    From the fiery battle-ground.

When I found a cheerful stranger,
    Calm, critical, serene,
Well sheltered from all danger,
    Painting a battle-scene.

He was cordially glad to see me —
    The coolly smiling wretch —
And inquired with admiration,
    " Do you mind if I make a sketch ? "

So he had me down in a minute,
    With murmurs of real delight ;
My " color " was " delicious,"
    My " action " was " just right ! "

And he prattled on with ardor
    Of the moving scene below ;
Of the " values " of the smoke-wreaths,
    And " the splendid rush and go "

THE MARCH.

Of the headlong desperate charges
  Where a thousand lives were spent;
Of the "massing" in the foreground
  With the "middle distance" blent.

Said I, "You speak serenely
  Of the living death in view.
These are human creatures dying —
  Are you not human too?

"This is a present battle,
  Where all men strive to-day.
How does it chance you sit apart?
  Which is your banner — say!"

His fresh cheek blanched a little,
  But he answered with a smile
That he fought not on either side;
  He was watching a little while.

"Watching!" said I, "and neutral!
  Neutral in times like these!"
And I plucked him off his sketching stool
  And brought him to his knees.

I stripped him of his travelling cloak
  And showed him to the sky:
By his uniform — a traitor!
  By his handiwork — a spy!

183

I dragged him back to the field he left;
To the fate he was fitted for.
We have no place for lookers on
When all the world 's at war !

THE OLD-TIME WAIL.

An Associated Press despatch describes the utterance of a Farmers' Alliance meeting in Kansas as consisting mostly of " the old-time wail of distress."

STILL Dives hath no peace. Broken his slumber,
His feasts are troubled, and his pleasures fail ;
For still he hears from voices without number
The same old wail.

They gather yet in field and town and city, —
The people, discontented, bitter, pale, —
And murmur of oppression, pain, and pity, —
The old-time wail.

And weary Dives, jaded in his pleasures,
Finding the endless clamor tiresome, stale —
Would gladly give a part of his wide treasures
To quiet that old wail.

Old ? Yes, as old as Egypt. Sounding lowly
From naked millions, in the desert hid,
Starving and bleeding while they builded, slowly,
The Pharaohs' pyramid.

As old as Rome. That endless empire's minions
    Raised ever and again the same dull 'cry;
And even Cæsar's eagle bent his pinions
      While it disturbed the sky.

As old as the Dark Ages. The lean peasant,
    Numerous, patient, still as time went by
Made his lord's pastimes something less than
    pleasant
      With that unceasing cry.

It grew in volume down the crowding ages;
    Unheeded still, and unappeased, it swelled.
And now it pleads in vain, and now it rages —
      The answer still withheld.

A century ago 'it shrieked and clamored
    Till trembled emperors and kings grew pale;
At gates of palaces it roared and hammered, —
      The same old wail.

It got no final answer, though its passion
    Altered the face of Europe, monarchs slew;
But ere it sank to silence, in some fashion
      Others were wailing, too.

And now in broad America we hear it, —
    From crowded street, from boundless hill and vale.
Hear, Dives! Have ye not some cause to fear it, —
      This old-time wail?

Louder, my brother! Let us wail no longer
    Like those past sufferers whose hearts did break.
We are a wiser race, a braver, stronger —
        Let us not ask, but take!

So Dives shall have no distress soever,
    No sound of anguished voice by land or sea;
The-old time wail shall so be stilled forever,
        And Dives shall not be!

FREE LAND IS NOT ENOUGH.

FREE land is not enough. In earliest days
When man, the baby, from the earth's bare breast
Drew for himself his simple sustenance,
Then freedom and his effort were enough.
The world to which a man is born to-day
Is a constructed, human, man-built world.
As the first savage needed the free wood,
We need the road, the ship, the bridge, the house,
The government, society, and church, —
These are the basis of our life to-day,
As much necessities to modern man
As was the forest to his ancestor.
To say to the new-born, " Take here your land;
In primal freedom settle where you will,
And work your own salvation in the world,"
Is but to put the last come upon earth

THE MARCH.

Back with the dim forerunners of his race
To climb the race's stairway in one life !
Allied society owes to the young —
The new men come to carry on the world —
Account for all the past, the deeds, the keys,
Full access to the riches of the earth.
Why? That these new ones may not be compelled,
Each for himself, to do our work again —
But reach their manhood even with to-day,
And gain to-morrow sooner. To go on —
To start from where we are and go ahead —
That is true progress, true humanity !

WHO IS TO BLAME?

Who was to blame in that old time
    Of the unnoticed groan,
When prisoners without proof of crime
Rotted in dungeons wet with slime,
    And died unknown?

When torture was a common thing,
    When fire could speak,
When the flayed wretch hung quivering,
And rack-strained tendons, string by string,
    Snapped with a shriek?

Is it the Headsman, following still
    The laws his masters give?

Is it the Church or King who kill?
Or just the People, by whose will
    Church, King, and Headsman live?

The People, bowing slavish knee
    With tribute fruits of earth;
The People, gathering to see
The stake, the axe, the gallows-tree,
    In brutal mirth!

The People, countenancing pain
    By willing presence there;
The People — you might shriek in vain,
Poor son of Abel or of Cain —
    The People did not care!

And now, in this fair age we 're in,
    Who is to blame?
When men go mad and women sin
Because the life they struggle in
    Enforces shame!

When torture is so deep, so wide —
    The kind we give —
So long drawn out, so well supplied,
That men die now by suicide,
    Rather than live!

Is it the Rich Man, grinding still
    The faces of the poor?

Is it our System which must kill?
Or just the People, by whose will
  That system can endure?

The People, bowing slavish knee
  With tribute fruits of earth;
The People, who can bear to see
In crime and death and poverty
  Fair ground for mirth!

The People, countenancing pain
  By willing presence there;
The People — you may shriek in vain —
Protest, rebel, beseech, complain —
  The People do not care!

Each man and woman feels the weight
  Of their own private share;
But for the suffering of the state,
That falls on all men soon or late,
  The People do not care!

IF A MAN MAY NOT EAT NEITHER CAN HE WORK.

How can he work? He never has been taught
  The free use of what faculties he had.
Why should he work? Who ever yet has thought
  To give a love of working to the lad.

How can he work? His life has felt the lack
  Of all that makes us work; the proud, the free,
Each saying to the world, "I give you back
  Part of the glory you have given me I"

Why should he work? He has no honor high,
  Born of great trust and wealth and sense of power;
Honor, that makes us yearn before we die
  To add our labor to the world's rich dower.

How can he work? He has no inner strength
  Urging him on to action, no desire
To strain and wrestle, to achieve at length,
  Burning in all his veins, — a hidden fire.

Why should he work? There is no debt behind
  That man's nobility most longs to pay;
No claim upon him, — only the one blind
  Brute instinct that his dinner lies that way.

And that is not enough. Who may not eat
  Freely at life's full table all his youth,
Can never work in power and joy complete,
  In fulness, and in honor, and in truth.

HIS OWN LABOR.

LET every man be given what he earns!
We cry, and call it justice. Let him have
The product of his labor — and no more!
190

Well, then, let us begin with life's first needs,
And give him of the earth what he can make;
As much of air and light as he can make,
As much of ocean, and sweet wind and rain,
And flowers, and grass, and fruit, as he can make.
But no, we answer this is mockery :
No man makes these things. But of human wealth
Let every man be given what he makes,
The product of his labor, and no more.
Ah, well ! So to the farmer let us give
Corn, and still corn, and only corn at last.
So to the grazier, meat; the fisher, fish;
Cloth to the weaver; to the mason, walls;
And let the writer sit and read his books —
The product of his labor — and naught else !
But no, we answer ! Still you laugh at us.
We mean not his own labor in that sense,
But his share in the work of other men.
As much of what they make as he can buy
In fair exchange for labor of his own.
So let it be. As much of life's rich fruit —
The product of the labor of the world —
As he can equal with his own two hands,
His own supply of energy and skill !
As much of Shakespeare, Homer, Socrates,
As much of Wagner, Beethoven, and Bach,
As much of Franklin, Morse, and Edison,
As much of Watt, and Stephenson and Bell,

Of Euclid, Aristotle, Angelo,
Columbus, Raleigh, and George Washington,
Of all the learning of our patient years,
Of all the peace and smoothness we have won,
Of all the heaped up sciences and arts,
And luxuries that man has ever made, —
He is to have what his own toil can match !
Or, passing even this, giving no thought
To this our heritage, our vast bequest,
Condemn him to no more of human help
From living men than he can give to them !
Toil of the soldiers on the western plains,
Toil of the hardened sailors on the sea,
Toil of the sweating ploughman in the field,
The engine-driver, digger in the mine,
And weary weaver in the roaring mill.
Of all the hands and brains and hearts that toil
To fill the world with riches day by day,
Shall he have naught of this but what one man
Can give return for from his own supply ?
Brother — There is no payment in the world !
We work and pour our labor at the feet
Of those who are around us and to come.
We live and take our living at the hands
Of those who are around us and have been.
No one is paid. No person can have more
Than he can hold. And none can do beyond
The power that 's in him. To each child that 's born

Belongs as much of all our human good
As he can take and use to make him strong.
And from each man, debtor to all the world,
Is due the fullest fruit of all his powers,
His whole life's labor, proudly rendered up,
Not as return — can moments pay an age?
But as the simple duty of a man.
Can he do less — receiving everything?

AS FLEW THE CROSS.

As flew the fiery cross from hand to hand,
Kindling the scattered people to one flame,
Out-blazing fiercely to a sudden war;
As beacon fires flamed up from hill to hill,
Crying afar to valleys hidden wide
To tell their many dwellers of a fear
That made them one — a danger shadowing all! —
So flies to-day the torch of living fire,
From mouth to mouth, from distant ear to ear;
And all the people of all nations hear;
The printed word, the living word that tells
Of the great glory of the coming day, —
The joy that makes us one forevermore!

TO LABOR.

SHALL you complain who feed the world?
　　Who clothe the world?
　　Who house the world?
Shall you complain who are the world,
　　Of what the world may do?
　　　　As from this hour
　　　　You use your power,
　　The world must follow you!

The world's life hangs on your right hand!
　　　Your strong right hand!
　　　Your skilled right hand!
You hold the whole world in your hand.
　　See to it what you do!
　　　　Or dark or light,
　　　　Or wrong or right,
　　The world is made by you!

Then rise as you never rose before!
　　　Nor hoped before!
　　　Nor dared before!
And show as was never shown before,
　　The power that lies in you!
　　　　Stand all as one!
　　　　See justice done!
　　Believe, and Dare, and Do!

HARDLY A PLEASURE.

SHE had found it dull in her city;
  So had they, in a different mob.
She travelled to look for amusement;
  They travelled to look for a job.

She was loaded with fruit and candy,
  And her section piled with flowers,
With magazine, novels, and papers
  To shorten the weary hours.

Her friends came down in a body
  With farewells merry and sweet,
And left her with laughter and kisses,
  On the broad plush-cushioned seat.

She was bored before she started,
  And the journey was dull and far.
" Travelling 's hardly a pleasure ! "
  Said the girl in the palace car.

———

Then they skulked out in the darkness
  And crawled in under the cars,
To ride on the trucks as best they might,
  To hang by the chains and bars.

None came to see their starting,
  And their friendliest look that day
Was that of a green young brakeman,
  Who looked the other way.

They were hungry before they started,
  With the hunger that turns to pain —
" Travelling 's hardly a pleasure,"
  Said the three men under the train.

She complained of the smoke and cinders,
  She complained of the noise and heat,
She complained of the table service,
  She complained of the things to eat.

She said it was so expensive,
  In spite of one's utmost care;
That feeing the porters and waiters
  Cost as much as a third-class fare.

That the seats were dirty and stuffy,
  That the berths were worse by far.
" Travelling 's hardly a pleasure I "
  Said the girl in the palace car.

They hung on in desperate silence,
  For a word was a tell-tale shout;
Their foul hats low on their bloodshot eyes,
  To keep the cinders out.

The dirt beat hard on their faces,
  The noise beat hard on their ears,
And a moment's rest to a straining limb
  Meant the worst of human fears.

THE MARCH.

They clutched and clung in the darkness
  While the stiffness turned to pain.
" Travelling 's hardly a pleasure,"
  Said the three men under the train.

She stepped airily out in the morning,
  When the porter had brushed her awhile.
She gave him a silver dollar;
  He gave her an ivory smile.

She complained to her friends that morning
  Of a most distressing dream :
" I thought I heard in the darkness
  A sort of a jolting scream !

" I thought I felt in the darkness
  The great wheels joggle and swing;
Travelling 's hardly a pleasure
  When you dream such a horrible thing ! "

They crept shuddering out in the morning,
  Red spots with the coal's black stain.
" Travelling 's hardly a pleasure ! "
  Said the two men under the train.

NATIONALISM.

THE nation is a unit.   That which makes
You an American of our to-day

Requires the nation and its history,
Requires the sum of all our citizens,
Requires the product of our common toil,
Requires the freedom of our common laws,
The common heart of our humanity.
Decrease our population, check our growth,
Deprive us of our wealth, our liberty,
Lower the nation's conscience by a hair,
And you are less than that you were before !
You stand here in the world the man you are
Because your country is America.
Our liberty belongs to each of us ;
The nation guarantees it ; in return
We serve the nation, serving so ourselves.
Our education is a common right ;
The state provides it, equally to all,
Each taking what he can, and in return
We serve the state, so serving best ourselves.
Food, clothing, all necessities of life, —
These are a right as much as liberty !
The nation feeds its children. In return
We serve the nation, serving still ourselves —
Nay, not ourselves — ourself ! We are but parts,
The unit is the state, — America.

THE KING IS DEAD! LONG LIVE THE KING!

WHEN man, the hunter, winning in the race,
Had conquered much, and, conquering, grown apace,
Till out of victory he found defeat,
And, having eaten all, had naught to eat, —
Then might some Jeremiah sad have said,
Seeing his hopeless case, " The King is dead ! "

But man is master most in power to change ;
He turned his forest to a cattle range ;
There was no foe to strive with — wherefore strive ?
No food to kill — he kept his food alive.
Herding his dinner, see him sit and sing
Serene, "The King is dead ! Long live the King ! "

When man the shepherd, after years did pass,
By nature's increase grew, until the grass
Failed to support the requisite supply
Of cattle who must live lest he should die ;
Again a grieved observer might be led
To pitifully say, " The King is dead ! "

But man, who turned his prey into a pet,
To outwit hunger, was not baffled yet ;
He 'd searched for grass so long he 'd learned to
    praise it,
And now that grass was short — why, he could
    raise it !

His dinner sprouted with the happy spring
Profuse, "The King is dead! Long live the King!"

When man, the farmer, growing very great,
Out of his children built the busy State,
Those greedy children, to his loud alarm,
Pinched all the profits off the old man's farm,
Killing the golden goose, and while he bled,
Cried sage economists, "The King is dead!"

But he, good sooth, was never more alive;
He watched the pools and trusts around him
    strive,
And when he 'd learned the trick — it was not
    long —
He organized himself — a million strong!
Cornered the food supply! A Farmer's Ring!
Hurrah! "The King is dead! Long live the King!"

"HOW MANY POOR!"

"Whene'er I take my walks abroad, how many
    poor I see!"
Said pious Watts, and thanked the Lord that not
    so poor was he.
I see so many poor to-day I think I 'll walk no more,
And then the poor in long array come knocking at
    my door.

The hungry poor! The dirty poor! The poor of
    evil smell!
Yet even these we could endure if they were only
    well!
But, O, this sick and crippled crew! The lame, the
    deaf, the blind!
What can a Christian person do with these upon
    his mind!
They keep diseases growing still like plants on
    greenhouse shelves,
And they 're so generous they will not keep them
    to themselves;
They propagate amazing crimes and vices scandal-
    ous,
And then at most uncertain times they wreak the
    same on us!
With charity we would prevent this poverty and
    woe,
But find the more we 've fondly spent, the more
    the poor do grow!
We 've tried by punishment full sore to mend the
    case they 're in;
The more we punish them the more they sin, and
    sin, and sin!
We make the punishment more kind, we give them
    wise reform,
And they, with a contented mind, flock to our
    prisons warm!

Then science comes with solemn air, and shows us
    social laws,
Explaining how the poor are there from a purely
    natural cause.
'T is natural for low and high to struggle and to
    strive;
'T is natural for the worse to die and the better to
    survive.
We swallowed all this soothing stuff, and easily
    were led
To think if we were stern enough, the poor would
    soon be dead.
But, O! in vain we squeeze, and grind, and drive
    them to the wall —
For all our deadly work we find it does not kill
    them all!
The more we struggle they survive! increase and
    multiply!
There seem to be more poor alive, in spite of all
    that die!
Whene'er I take my walks abroad how many poor
    I see,
And eke at home! How long, O Lord! How long
    must this thing be!

THE DEAD LEVEL.

THERE is a fear among us as we strive,
  As we succeed or fail, or starve or revel,
That there will be no pleasure left alive
When we in peace and joy at last arrive
  At one dead level.

And still the strangest part of this strange fear
  Is that it is not for ourselves we fear it.
We wish to rise and gain; we look ahead
To pleasant years of peace ere we are dead;
  We wish that peace, but wish no other near it!

Say, does it spoil your pleasure in a town
  To have your neighbors' gardens full of roses?
Is your house dearer when its eye looks down
On evil-smelling shanties rough and brown?
  Is your nose safer than your neighbor's nose is?

Are you unhappy at some noble fête
  To see the whole bright throng in radiant dresses?
Is your State safer when each other State
That borders it is full of want and hate?
  Peace must be peace to all before it blesses.

Is knowledge sweeter when it is hemmed in
  By ignorance that does not know its master?
Is goodness easier when plenteous sin
Surrounds it? And can you not win
  Joy for yourself without your friend's disaster?

O foolish children ! With more foolish fear,
　Unworthy even of a well-trained devil !
Good things are good for all men, — that is clear ;
To doubt it shows your heads are nowhere near
　To that much-dreaded level !

THE CART BEFORE THE HORSE.

OUR business system has its base
On one small thought that 's out of place ;
　The merest trifle — nothing much, of course.
The truth is there — who says it 's not ?
Only — the trouble is — you 've got
　　The cart before the horse !

You say unless a man shall work
Right earnestly, and never shirk,
　He may not eat. Now look — the change is small,
And yet the truth is plain to see —
Unless man eats, and frequently,
　　He cannot work at all !

And which comes first ! Why, that is plain,
The man comes first. And, look again —
　A baby ! with an appetite to fit !
You have to feed him years and years,
And train him up with toil and tears,
　　Before he works a bit !

So let us change our old ideas,
And learn with these advancing years
To give the oats before we ask for speed;
Not set the hungry horse to run,
And tell him when the race is done
That he shall have his feed!

THE AMŒBOID CELL.

SAID the Specialized Cell to the Amœboid Cell,
"Why don't you develop like me?
Just combine with the others,
Unite with your brothers,
And grow to a thing you can see, —
An organized creature like me!"

Said the Amœboid Cell to the Specialized Cell,
"But where would my liberty be?
If I 'm one with a class,
I should lose in the mass
All my Individualitee!
And that is a horror to me!"

Said the Specialized Cell to the Amœboid Cell,
"What good does it do you to-day?
You 're amorphous and small,
You 've no organs at all,
You can't even get out of the way!
You don't half understand what I say!"

Said the Amœboid Cell to the Specialized Cell,
   " But I 'm independent and free!
      I can float as I please
      In these populous seas,
   I 'm not fastened to anybodes !
   I have personal freedom, you see !

" And when I want organs and members and such,
   I project them, — an arm or a wing ;
      I can change as I will,
      But you have to keep still —
   Just a part of the mass where you cling !
   You never can be but one thing ! "

Said the Specialized Cell to the Amœboid Cell,
   " What you say is undoubtedly true,
      But I 'd rather be part
      Of a thing with a heart
   Than the whole of a creature like you !
   A memberless morsel like you !

" You say you 're immortal and separate and free,
   Yet you 've died by the billion before ;
      Just a speck in the slime
      At the birthday of time,
   And you never can be any more !
   As you are, you 've no future in store !

" You say you can be many things in yourself,
  Yet you 're all just alike to the end !
  I am part of a whole —
  Of a thing with a soul —
  And the whole is the unit, my friend !
  But that you can scarce comprehend !

" You are only yourself, — just a series of ones ;
  You can only say ' I ' — never ' we ' ;
  All of us are combined
  In a creature with mind,
  And *we* are the creature you see !
  And the creature feeds *us* — which is *me !*

" And being combined in a body like that
  It can wisely provide us with food ;
  And we vary and change
  In a limitless range ;
  We are specialized now, for our good !
  And we each do our work — as we should !

" What protection have you from the chances of
    Fate ?
  What provision have you for the morrow ?
  You get food when it drops,
  And you die when it stops !
  You can't give or take, lend or borrow !
  You helpless free-agent of sorrow ! "

Just then came a frost, and the Amœboid Cell
  Died out by the billion again;
    But the Specialized Cell
    In the body felt well
  And rejoiced in his place in the brain !
  The dead level of life with a brain !

THE SURVIVAL OF THE FITTEST.

In northern zones the ranging bear
Protects himself with fat and hair.
Where snow is deep, and ice is stark,
And half the year is cold and dark,
He still survives a clime like that
By growing fur, by growing fat.
These traits, O Bear, which thou transmittest,
Prove the survival of the fittest !

To polar regions, waste and wan,
Comes the encroaching race of man ;
A puny, feeble little lubber,
He had no fur, he had no blubber.
The scornful bear sat down at ease
To see the stranger starve and freeze ;
But, lo ! the stranger slew the bear,
And ate his fat, and wore his hair !
These deeds, O Man, which thou committest,
Prove the survival of the fittest !

In modern times the millionaire
Protects himself as did the bear.
Where Poverty and Hunger are,
He counts his bullion by the car.
Where thousands suffer, still he thrives,
And after death his will survives.
The wealth, O Crœsus, thou transmittest
Proves the survival of the fittest !

But, lo ! some people, odd and funny,
Some men without a cent of money,
The simple common Human Race,
Chose to improve their dwelling-place.
They had no use for millionaires;
They calmly said the world was theirs ;
They were so wise, so strong, so many —
The millionaire ? There was n't any !
These deeds, O Man, which thou committest,
Prove the survival of the fittest !

DIVISION OF PROPERTY.

SOME sailors were starving at sea
On a raft where they happened to be,
        When one of the crew
        Who was hidden from view
Was found to be feasting most free.

Then they cursed him in language profane,
Because there on the pitiless main
    While the others did starve,
    He could ladle and carve,
Eating food which they could not obtain.

"But," said he, " 't is my own little store !
To feed all of you would take more !
    If I shared, 't would be found
    That it would not go round ;
And you all would starve on as before !

" It would only prolong your distress
To distribute this one little mess !
    The supply is so small
    I had best eat it all,
For me it will comfort and bless ! "

This reasoning sounded most fair,
But the men had large appetites there,
    And while he explained
    They ate all that remained,
Forgetting to leave out his share !

CHRISTIAN VIRTUES.

Oh, dear !
The Christian virtues will disappear !
Nowhere on land or sea

Will be room for charity !
Nowhere, in field or city,
A person to help or pity !
Better for them, no doubt,
Not to need helping out
Of their old miry ditch.
But, alas for us, the rich !
For we shall lose, you see,
Our boasted charity ! —
Lose all the pride and joy
Of giving the poor employ,
And money, and food, and love
(And making stock thereof !).
Our Christian virtues are gone,
With nothing to practise on !

It don't hurt them a bit,
For they can't practise it ;
But it 's our great joy and pride —
What virtue have we beside ?
We believe, as sure as we live,
That it is more blessed to give
Than to want, and waste, and grieve,
And occasionally receive !
And here are the people pressing
To rob us of our pet blessing !
No chance to endow or bedizen
A hospital, school, or prison,

And leave our own proud name
To Gratitude and Fame !
No chance to do one good deed,
To give what we do not need,
To leave what we cannot use
To those whom we deign to choose !
When none want broken meat,
How shall our cake be sweet ?
When none want flannels and coals,
How shall we save our souls ?
Oh, dear !   Oh, dear !
The Christian virtues will disappear !

The poor have their virtues rude, —
Meekness and gratitude,
Endurance, and respect
For us, the world's elect ;
Economy, self-denial,
Patience in every trial,
Self-sacrifice, self-restraint, —
Virtues enough for a saint !
Virtues enough to bear
All this life's sorrow and care !
Virtues by which to rise
To a front seat in the skies !
How can they turn from this
To common earthly bliss, —
Mere clothes, and food, and drink,

And leisure to read and think,
And art, and beauty, and ease, —
There is no crown for these !
True, if their gratitude
Were not for fire and food,
They might still learn to bless
The Lord for their happiness !
And, instead of respect for wealth,
Might learn from beauty, and health,
And freedom in power and pelf,
Each man to respect himself !
And, instead of scraping and saving,
Might learn from using and having
That man's life should be spent
In a grand development !
But this is petty and small ;
These are not virtues at all ;
They do not look as they should ;
They don't do *us* any good !
Oh, dear ! Oh, dear ! Oh, dear !
The Christian virtues will disappear !

WHAT 'S THAT?

I MET a little person on my land,
  A-fishing in the waters of my stream ;
He seemed a man, yet could not understand
  Things that to most men very simple seem.

"Get off!" said I; "this land is mine, my friend!
Get out!" said I; "this brook belongs to me!
I own the land, and you must make an end
Of fishing here so free.

"I own this place, the land and water too!
You have no right to be here, that is flat!
Get off it! That is all I ask of you! — "
"Own it?" said he; "what 's that?"

"What 's that?" said I, "why, that is common sense!
I own the water and the fishing right;
I own the land from here to yonder fence;
Get off, my friend, or fight!"

He looked at the clear stream so neatly kept;
He looked at teeming vine and laden tree,
And wealthy fields of grain that stirred and slept;
"I see!" he cried, "I see!

"You mean you cut the wood and plowed the field,
From your hard labor all this beauty grew,
To you is due the richness of the yield;
You have some claim, 't is true."

"Not so," said I, with manner very cool,
And tossed my purse into the air and caught it;
"Do I look like a laborer, you fool?
It 's mine because I bought it!"

Again he looked as if I talked in Greek,
    Again he scratched his head and twirled his hat,
Before he mustered wit enough to speak.
    "Bought it?" said he, "what's that?"

And then he said again, "I see! I see!
    You mean that some men toiled with plows and
        hoes,
And while those worked for you, you toiled with glee
    At other work for those."

"Not so!" said I, getting a little hot,
    Thinking the man a fool as well as funny;
"I'm not a working-man, you idiot;
    I bought it with my money!"

And still that creature stared and dropped his jaw,
    Till I could have destroyed him where he sat.
"Money," said I, "money, and moneyed law!"
    "Money?" said he, "what's that?"

AN ECONOMIST.

THE serene savage sitting in his tree
    Saw empires rise and fall,
And moralized on their uncertainty.
    (He never rose at all!)

He was full fat from god-sent droves of prey;
    He was full calm from satisfied desire;
He was full wise in that he chose to stay
    Free from ambition's fire.

"See," quoth the savage, "how they toil and strive
 To make things better, — vain and idle wish!
Here is good store of what keeps man alive,
  Of fruit, and flesh, and fish.

"Poor discontented wretches, fed on air,
 Seeking to change the normal lot of man,
To lure him from this natural strife and care,
  With vague Utopian plan!

"Here 's wealth and joy — why seek for any change?
 Why labor for a more elaborate life?
As if God could not his own world arrange
  Without our fretful strife!

"Those who complain of savagery as low
 Are merely proven lazy, and too weak
To live by skilful hunt and deadly blow;
  It is their needs that speak.

"Complain of warfare! Cry that peace is sweet!
 Complain of hunting! Prate of toil and trade!
It only proves that they cannot compete
  In the free life we 've made."

Another empire reeled into its grave;
 The savage sat serenely as before,
As calm and wise, as cunning and as brave —
  Never an atom more.

CHARITY.

CAME two young children to their mother's shelf
 (One was quite little, and the other big),
And each in freedom calmly helped himself.
  (One was a pig.)

The food was free and plenty for them both,
 But one was rather dull and very small;
So the big smarter brother, nothing loath,
  He took it all.

At which the little fellow raised a yell
 Which tired the other's more æsthetic ears;
He gave him here a crust, and there a shell
  To stop his tears.

He gave with pride, in manner calm and bland,
 Finding the other's hunger a delight;
He gave with piety — his full left hand
  Hid from his right.

He gave and gave — O blessed Charity!
 How sweet and beautiful a thing it is!
How fine to see that big boy giving free
  What is not his!